# A TRUCE THAT IS NOT PEACE

# Also by Miriam Toews

NOVELS
*Fight Night*
*Women Talking*
*All My Puny Sorrows*
*Irma Voth*
*The Flying Troutmans*
*A Complicated Kindness*
*A Boy of Good Breeding*
*Summer of My Amazing Luck*

NONFICTION
*Swing Low: A Life*

# A TRUCE THAT IS NOT PEACE

# MIRIAM TOEWS

BLOOMSBURY PUBLISHING

NEW YORK · LONDON · OXFORD · NEW DELHI · SYDNEY

BLOOMSBURY PUBLISHING
Bloomsbury Publishing Inc.
1359 Broadway, New York, NY 10018, USA
50 Bedford Square, London, WC1B 3DP, UK
Bloomsbury Publishing Ireland Limited,
29 Earlsfort Terrace, Dublin 2, D02 AY28, Ireland

BLOOMSBURY, BLOOMSBURY PUBLISHING and the Diana logo
are trademarks of Bloomsbury Publishing Plc

First published in 2025 in Canada by Alfred A. Knopf Canada
First published in the United States by Bloomsbury Publishing in 2025

Copyright © Miriam Toews, 2025

All rights reserved. No part of this publication may be: i) reproduced or transmitted in any form, electronic or mechanical, including photocopying, recording, or by means of any information storage or retrieval system without prior permission in writing from the publishers; or ii) used or reproduced in any way for the training, development, or operation of artificial intelligence (AI) technologies, including generative AI technologies. The rights holders expressly reserve this publication from the text and data mining exception as per Article 4(3) of the Digital Single Market Directive (EU) 2019/790.

ISBN: 978-1-63973-474-0 (hardcover); 9781-63973-475-7 (ebook);
978-1-63973-885-4 (hardcover signed edition)

Library of Congress Cataloging-in-Publication Data is available

2 4 6 8 10 9 7 5 3 1

Text design by Kelly Hill
Typeset by Sean Tai
Printed in the United States by Lakeside Book Company

To find out more about our authors and books visit www.bloomsbury.com
and sign up for our newsletters.

Bloomsbury books may be purchased for business or promotional use.
For information on bulk purchases please contact Macmillan Corporate and
Premium Sales Department at specialmarkets@macmillan.com.
For product safety–related questions contact productsafety@bloomsbury.com.

*To Marj.*

"... we might remember the dead without being haunted by them, give to our lives a coherence that is not 'closure,' and learn to live with our memories, our families, and ourselves amid a truce that is not peace."
—Christian Wiman

# One

April 2023

I've agreed to join a "Conversación" in Mexico City. This is not really a conversation but an event where a series of writers from all over the world read a story or an essay or *a thing* they've written on a specific subject, a subject determined by the Conversación Comité in Mexico City. The subject this time is "Why do I write?"

I've replied to the Director of the Conversación: Why do I write? Or . . . Why write?

Why do I write, he said.

⁓

"The Russian loves recalling life, but he does not love living."

—Anton Chekhov

⁓

December 28, 1995

Dear Marj,

I have my little Buddha reminding me to be kind, my red-and-black half-moon reminding me of the instability of the universe, my rose-coloured curtain to create a mood of wonder, my rose-scented incense to lull me to sleep, but still . . . I am so confused, angry, sad (overwhelmingly, close to tears fifty times a day), unproductive, vengeful, snide, lonely, LONELY, most of all, so fucking lonely. But what do I do about it? Read, read, read more and more, never go out, stare at my computer, piss off C with what he thinks are terminal neuroses, say yeah yeah yeah to the kids, dream of getting drunk every night, never do.

What the fuck is my problem?

We're BROKE, BROKE, BROKE—a piddle of grant dough will come in, then we're dead.

I hate writing—what a crock of shit, blah blah blah. I'm eating myself. The house is falling apart. I'm bleeding, I'm hemorrhaging, my organs are slipping out of me, dark-red tissue—is it my liver?—like pieces of rotting watermelon. It's 10 p.m. and I'm wearing flannel pajamas with small blue tulips on them.

Little G is sculpting cats out of clay, and she asks me if I'm ever afraid.

"Punishment, perhaps, or some contagion of fate,
    finds her here,
her hair shorn, both wrists wrapped, her eyes open,
pondering the parable of perfect silence."
—Christian Wiman

"You see, there is nothing for me to do here anymore. I am embarking because I am bored, because I am frightened, because I am sad. But really because I don't find my jokes funny anymore. Looking back over them I ask myself if they were ever funny, or did I just make them so by my laughter."
—Sam Savage

~

November 2022

An email from my mother in the Toronto Western Hospital, to me while I was on a trip to Rome:

Yes Mir, here I am. Doing well, no pain. Still more assessing today. I made quite a turmoil at 2 a.m. Woke up, walked towards the bathroom and accidentally pulled some tubing. Well, I was there, naked, a huge puddle of blood on the floor. I managed to stop the bleeding, pulled a chair over to sit down and waited. My neighbour walked by and said she would get help. So she walked off with her IV. After what seemed like a lengthy wait the nurse arrived, looked at me and said, Oh. First order of the day was to clean up the blood. Then eventually she got to me. Calmly cleaned up my bed, then my vein line, gave me a chance to go pee and got me back into bed. Another nurse came along to check my b.p. Said, Don't laugh, finally got a reading, just a little high. I went back to sleep, and she went back to her desk. Well, here I am right as rain and ready for a new day.

P.S. It really was funny. You just stay where you are and enjoy it. I'll definitely let you know as soon as I know if anything develops.

Hey, I love you! Have fun. Chow!
Mom

⁓

"One remembers one's first love as one remembers the first casualty of war."

—Pushkin

⁓

I had that dream again, the one where I'm being shot in the face at close range and my mouth is flying off down some white corridor, and I'm so angry with myself for not getting out of the way in time.

My partner E said last evening: I know you people (meaning, my family) don't talk about your pain; you just kill yourselves. My daughter G and I were impressed with the genuine comic worth of that statement.

(Another impressive moment from E: Once, when speaking about my exes, he referred to them as my backlist.)

And what is the white corridor in my dream? A narrow spit of land? Is it the act of writing? A thing between life and death? From life, against death—writing? A sort of ledge? A high-up ledge, just wide enough for a smallish foot or hand to hold on to, but easy to drop from. A death-defying ledge?

Awake in the night, I heard my neighbour screaming alone in the back lane. I'll bring this iron bar down on your fucking face! I. Hate. You.

I lay in my dark bedroom, sinking into my memory foam, and nodded, calmly.

∽

A skunk with distemper, who may have lived under our back deck for years until we did renovations, keeps returning to our house and falling blindly into the window well, where it becomes trapped. The city says the skunk is too deranged to understand how not to keep coming back and falling into the same trap.

Meanwhile, I have been finding it very difficult to generate interest from others in my idea of a Wind Museum.

And I've been seeing a Russian Jungian shrink. I haven't yet told her about the Wind Museum.

I read online that the greatest fear therapists have is that their client will commit suicide. Having read that—stupidly, because why am I reading about the fears of therapists—I begin every session of ours, mine and my therapist's, with a disclaimer: I'm not suicidal, don't worry. And then I talk and talk and talk about suicide.

In conventional therapy the patient, or "client," moves forward from A to B to C. But the Zen Buddhist idea is that we can stay at A for as long as we want, and if we stay at A long enough B will come looking for *us*.

The young fruit vendor in Paris tenderly placing a Bing cherry into the palm of an old woman who eats it on the spot, no words exchanged.

The young minders in Marseille out walking with their old women on the high church promenade, the church at the top of the city, the old women dressed in their best dresses, hats, handbags, canes, staring at their city, at the sea, thinking . . . what? The young minders staring at their phones and eager to move on, walking too fast, dragging the old women, who find it hard to keep up, their canes out of sync with their steps.

So, says my Russian Jungian shrink, you were born . . . ?

Last year a derecho blew through town on my birthday, at noon. It turned the sky green, brought down trees and hydro lines, smashed windows, scattered pylons and garbage, tipped cars, knocked cyclists off their bikes, and forced me to pick up my four-year-old grandson and run as fast as I could for shelter in the 7-Eleven near our home. The cashier told us to stay away from the glass door. The skunk with distemper stayed safe, trapped in our window well.

Is it so obvious? My dream of being shot in the face?

Who is the shooter?

*Horacio Quiroga.* A small glass of cyanide.

*Ryūnosuke Akutagawa.* Barbital. It was said he had a "vague insecurity" about the future.

*Manuel Acuña Navarro.* A glass of cyanide. It is thought he drank the poison "because of a woman." It is said that tears welled up in his closed eyes, as he'd once described in his own poem.

⸺

On that day many years ago, my mother finally convinced my father to order a ham sandwich. It was the last time she would see him, although she didn't know that. He ordered the sandwich to make her happy.

You have to eat something, Mel!

But why would he need to eat?

We sat at a long table at a family restaurant in Winnipeg called Tubby's. The restaurant is not there anymore. My son was eleven years old and bored with this family dinner. He wanted to leave to meet his friends and shoot hoops. I watched my father watching my son loping down the sidewalk, leaving, with not a single glance backwards. My father's eyes were *trained* on him. Long minutes, long sidewalk, long table.

He chatted about colours with my daughter G, his eight-year-old granddaughter.

Why purple?

I just like it.

My father didn't touch his ham sandwich. He smiled and looked out the window at the long sidewalk and talked about colours. If I'd had the idea of the Wind Museum then, I would have told him and G that a derecho can turn the sky green in seconds.

⁓

In Athens, near the Parthenon, I saw a boy and his father standing on a gravel path and staring at a man in a wheelchair. The boy picked up a handful of tiny stones and threw them at the man in the wheelchair. His father laughed and put his arm around the boy.

The beginning and the end.

So . . . you were born? prompts my shrink.

Well, yeah. I was conceived on the night of my grandfather's funeral. He was an egg farmer. Imagine handling eggs all your life. It might have been better for him if he'd been a bushwhacker like my other grandfather, just whaling away at trees, knocking them down, chainsawing them to dust, chopping them to shreds. But this grandfather, my father's father, had to be so careful as an egg farmer. It was the wrong profession for him. Stress had eaten away at his stomach until it was gone, and he starved to death.

My father was destroyed by grief over this. He was going out of his mind. So, the conception was a desperate thing, as far as I can tell. From what my mother told me. To escape a broken heart, to support the idea of life and to ward off death and morbidity.

My mother wouldn't have described it that way. She said, That night? That night he was either going to kill himself or create a new life.

That's how I came to be. My mother had prayed for six years to become pregnant again. Had she considered avenues other than prayer? That was my older sister's joke. And when I came along, finally, they gave me an old name from the Bible that means bitter and rebellious.

I screamed non-stop the entire first year of my life. And my father stopped talking for that entire year. He was completely silent, like a mime—but without miming. He would forget that I'd been born. My mother would point at me, tell him, The baby is here. Look, I am *holding* the baby. She's in my arms, can't you see? Sometimes my mother would flee to the neighbour's house to cry at their kitchen table, leaving me screaming alone behind the bars of my crib. My father remained utterly silent.

I had a terrible rash all over my body. I was allergic to milk. I was bright red, and I bit myself and clawed my arms and face and pulled my hair out. My parents thought I was mentally "retarded" (the term they used at that time). Well, they had wanted me, they had prayed for me. It was me or death. And they got me: conceived from death and despair and six years of begging God and born on the hottest day on record in my town. I moved into my new home, a little Hades. My mother and father couldn't see me or make out my features or my gender, there was so much sweat in their eyes—and tears—blinding them. But I existed, with my biblical name, irate and brooding.

In my town, when I was young, every home had a Daily Devotional calendar in their kitchen. Three hundred and sixty-five pages, each with their own bit of cribbed and vaguely biblical advice for the day. These weren't wall calendars; they were in the shape of small boxes and sat smugly on counters and tabletops. Every morning I'd rush out of bed to be the first to rip the day's page off, crumple it into a ball and shoot it into the garbage can under the sink. I kept a mental tally of my scores and stats and strove to break my record every single day. It was important to me that the page tore away in one clean piece, perfectly, from the perforated edge, and that my throw into the garbage can was nicely arced and not a bank shot. I used only one hand, my right hand, for each step of the process, which was meant to be fluid and quick. Tear, crumple, shoot.

Eventually I realized that nobody, not my parents or my sister, ever noticed or cared. Not a single one of us had ever *read* the Daily Devotional, our "One Minute with God." Would it have made a difference? At the dinner table one year, my mother asked me what I wanted for Christmas, and I answered emphatically, The Daily Devotional! My family laughed and laughed.

Our first major family holiday, organized by my jubilant mother when I was twelve, was in the Ecuadorian Amazon jungle, where we were robbed at gunpoint, threatened with death by machete, dive-bombed by vampire bats, had our flesh *culled* by multiple schools of piranhas ("culled" was the word my sister noted in her journal) and were force-fed guinea pigs.

A note in the margin of my sister's Ecuador Trip notebook: *What is mom up to?*

When we were robbed my sister was mortified that our father hadn't understood what was happening, was more troubled by his dorky Dad-style bumbling than the idea of being shot to death.

Honey? said my mother, taking over. We're being robbed now, okay? Give this fellow your wallet.

My sister in her notebook: *I've never been so embarrassed in my life.*

Another summer, my mother arranged for the four of us to have a picnic on a small uninhabited island in Falcon Lake. We set off in our tiny, nine-horsepower aluminum boat, my father steering with his hand on the motor, my sister in the prow, peering out ahead, acting as a spotter for rocks and other hard things we might collide with, and my mother and me huddled together on the middle bench.

Later that afternoon, our boat disappeared. When we'd arrived at the island my father had hauled it up onto the beach, well enough out of the water that it could be lodged firmly there in the sand. Now, it was gone. We four stood in a neat row on the beach, our hands visors blocking the sun, as though we were saluting an invisible major general, peering out at the water, the boat nowhere to be seen.

My mother began to laugh, and then my sister and I, and finally, my father.

> "It is ignominious to wage a confetti war against an utterly ruthless enemy."
> —Major General Sir Edward Louis Spears

Sitzkrieg, the phony war, the sitting war, the confetti war. The British dropped thirteen tons of paper leaflets over Germany to convince them the Nazis were evil. It didn't work.

Writing vs.?

Futile.

Speaking of futile. My first job after graduating from journalism school was as "traffic girl" for the tiniest radio station in the province of Manitoba. The station was a four-by-six cinder-block structure, no windows, with an antenna on top, in the middle of a wheat field next to the Perimeter Highway. There wasn't much traffic. My job was to get up early, at 5 a.m., listen to another radio station's traffic report, and then call in to my tiny station and say exactly the same thing. Maybe change a word or two. For example, Watch out for exhaust fog at the intersections. I'd add random words. Phrases like "my man." Or I'd say, Traffic is heeeeeeeaaaavy.

When I got hired for the job the manager asked me what my name was, and when I told him he said, No, no way, that's a crazy name, you're gonna be Lisa Cook. He told me to sign off with: And that's your traffic report, folks. I'm Lisa Cook.

My kids were little then. They were asleep at that hour, and it was so dark and quiet, and I loved it, forty below outside, wind howling. I'd like to install that exact wind in my museum—the wind with that time alone, the windows rattling, sitting on the couch in my pajamas, calling in the traffic report and using a fake name, adding words. The fog is baaaaaaaad, my man.

Once, I signed off with, "Let's move it, move it, move it in a love direction."

Finding your voice is different from hearing voices in your head. Or it isn't. Lisa Cook didn't last.

The narrow corridor. The spit of land. The confetti war. The beginning and the end. The Wind Museum, the derecho, the green sky, the head-shrinkers, the broken glass, the ledge.

~

My four-year-old grandson calls his one-year-old brother a fucking noodle head, and now I am the one who's in trouble for laughing.

Yes, I told my grandson on another occasion, it's true. I ate an entire church bulletin one Sunday out of sheer, excruciating boredom.

Are you telling him to eat paper? asked my daughter.

I'm telling him to beware of organized religion.

I think about my older sister. Raucous laughter and bewildering silence, like my father. Two gears, first and fourth, my mother said. But there were times in between those gears. My sister spent time in second and third gear, too. I watched her closely. But closely enough?

My daughter and mother and I recently opened my sister's cedar chest. We found notebooks and journals. One notebook began with an inspirational quote from Goethe: *Whatever you can do, or dream you can, begin it. Boldness has genius, power, and magic in it.* The writing on the notebook's last page was: Medical does (spelling mistake) of quar, no air, hard to breathe, scratching, allergies, pain, corticosteroids, beta blockers, salbutamol, bioflavonoids, change or addiction, 5 adrenergic, atrocent, mast cell stabilizers, no relief.

But between the beginning and the end of civilization, the Parthenons and the pelting of stones, is the narrow corridor, the spit of land, where writing lives. After disillusion—but just after—and before the end of relief—but quite a bit before—is where writing lives, where the soul (douchebag word, *soul*? Recently a private equity investor asked me if I thought I had a soul, and I couldn't stop laughing) of the writer floats, not as in a regatta, sun sparkling on water, but so precariously.

Or: in that space or spit of land or corridor, the silence of my sister, the suffering that destroyed her language, or destroyed language, or destroyed faith in language's ability to communicate anything of the human soul, or of her soul, it's all wind, the unmaking of her world, of the world—and in that space or spot of land or corridor is her asking me to write, to re-make my world, her world, the world. But who cares what this wind is called? I care. I don't care. I care. In that gap the effort is being made. And in that effort, but not in its outcome, is the creative act and where lies life. My sister's silence was a creative act—or was it? Had her suffering destroyed her language, or faith in language, and left her unable or unwilling to speak? Or was her silence a creative choice, an act of creation, an effort? Or was it language, or its futility, its shortcomings, that destroyed her first.

My sister and I singing our hearts out, aged twelve and six, as a birthday gift to our dad who was about to become the same age as Jesus had been when he was murdered. We had rehearsed hard and earnestly. We sang the song "I Don't Know How to Love Him" from the soundtrack of *Jesus Christ Superstar*. The song is from the point of view of a prostitute, but my sister and I didn't know that. We thought it was simply about Jesus, whom we knew our Dad really liked and related to.

*And I've had so many men before . . .*

Our mother was unable to contain herself. She could not stop laughing. She tried, but she couldn't.

My sister, offended, stopped playing and stormed off, a mighty wind, and left me there alone to sing the remaining verses of a plaintive prostitute.

"Love is the sacred name for loneliness."
—Christian Wiman

"Sometimes the mind thinks more about zwieback than about language and the like."
—Robert Walser

I tell my son-in-law a story: When my great-grandfather's wife dropped dead of an aneurysm on the kitchen floor, she left behind four kids. Shortly afterwards, my great-grandfather eloped with his seventeen-year-old housekeeper, who had recently been removed from his employ and locked up in her bedroom by her father, who feared this very thing happening. My great-grandfather had twelve more kids.

My son-in-law says, That makes sixteen kids.

And an angry father-in-law, I say.

My son-in-law understands why I told him this story. He smiles. Gotcha, he says. May I go?

∽

Thirty-eight years ago, the biological father of my son wrote a letter to my father. He wanted my father to know that he had asked me to marry him many times but that I'd refused every time. He had done his best to do the right thing. Now, he had to leave. He had to disappear into the Pacific Rim. He'd tried everything to get me to listen to reason but it hadn't worked. He had to go.

My father kept the letter, opened or unopened, read or unread—we don't know—for ten years, without mentioning it to anyone. Then, my father killed himself. My sister and I sat on either side of my mother on the couch in my living room and told her, He's gone.

My sister stored all my father's "paperwork" in her basement. She kept that letter, written to my father by my son's biological father, for ten years. We don't know if she read it or not. Then, my sister killed herself. I told my mother over the phone from Toronto, She's gone.

My sister's partner kept the letter in his basement for ten years. Then he met another woman and decided to move. He needed to clean out the basement and sell his house. One morning, he gave my sister's "paperwork," which included my father's "paperwork," to my mother.

That afternoon my mother read the letter written thirty-five years before by the biological father of my son to my father, and instantly tore it up. "There was no reason for that letter to exist," she said. "There was nothing edifying about it."

First order of the day. Clean up the blood.

Kept ten years by my father, kept ten years by my sister, kept ten years by my sister's partner. Destroyed in one second by my mother, its shreds tossed into the garbage can under the sink. We laughed.

Numbers and letters.

⁓

Many years ago, I stood next to the Assiniboine River and contemplated suicide, but only got as far as throwing my cellphone into the water before being talked away from the shore. Shortly after, I was visiting my psychiatrist at the Victoria Hospital in Winnipeg. I was terrified and gaunt and silent. I smoked cigarette after cigarette. I imagined every sort of bug trapped in the torn lining of my winter jacket. I was convinced that I had destroyed the people I loved most in the world.

An orderly walked past the room where my psychiatrist and I were sitting, and then walked past again. This time he stopped and put his head in the doorway. He asked me if I was who I am. No, I said. I'm Lisa Cook.

~

My father's last meal was an uneaten ham sandwich, and his last joke was directed at me: Did you have much trouble deciding what to wear?

I had worn the same torn jeans and green hoodie every day for the two weeks leading up to his death. Earlier, my father and I had eaten breakfast in a truck stop at Deacon's Corner, on the outskirts of Winnipeg. We were on our way into the city to meet with his doctor, and then to gather with the rest of the family for dinner at Tubby's where my father ordered a ham sandwich as a favour to my mother, and talked about colours with my daughter, and watched long and hard as my son ambled off home, getting smaller and smaller until he was a tiny dot and then gone.

If I combine the name of my father's favourite hymn with the name of my sister's favourite book at age eighteen, the title would be "Oh for a Thousand Tongues to Sing the Lives of Girls and Women."

If I then added another favourite book of my sister's and a favourite song of my mom's, the title would be "Oh for a Thousand Tongues to Sing the Lives of Girls and Women, Sons and Lovers in a Dangerous Time."

# A TRUCE THAT IS NOT PEACE

⤳

In Winnipeg, when I was pregnant with my son, I lived in an old apartment block by the Assiniboine River (the same river that years later would consume my cellphone) next to a tennis court and a bridge. An old woman lived down the hall from us. There were tiny little doors on our bigger doors. These tiny doors were the size and shape of a Penguin Classic and had little latches at eye level. When there was a knock on our door, we opened our tiny door first to see who it was and whether we wanted to open the bigger door to let them in. Many times each day, and sometimes during the night, the old woman would bang on my door, anguished, calling out for her son: Peter, Peter! She spoke only Hungarian. She was in the very late stages of dementia. Her words sounded like, Pater, Pater!

Her son, also old in my mind—I was twenty-one—lived alone in the apartment next to mine. He was a physics professor at the university. I would open my door and take the woman's hand and lead her to her son's door and knock and wait for him to open his door. He never bothered opening his tiny door with the latch to see who was there. He knew who was there. Here's your mom, I'd say. Peter would apologize, and I'd wave it away, and Peter would take his mother's hand and slowly walk her back down the dim corridor to her own apartment. Pater, Pater, Mama, Mama, the two would murmur, the old woman calm now and slumped against her old son's body.

One morning—it was late in the fall, after an appointment with my obstetrician—I came home to find police in the hallway outside my apartment. The door to Peter's apartment was open. The police held their hands over their faces when they spoke to me. Peter had electrocuted himself in the bathtub. I ran to my apartment and opened all the windows. I threw up in the kitchen sink. I went back into the hallway and said to the police, But what about his mother? She lives in the apartment down the hall. The police said they had taken her away.

I did not ask, but often wondered, which of these cataclysmic events happened first: Peter's death or his mother's removal?

ӭ

These days, my two youngest grandchildren have a habit of biting their mothers, and in some instances, other children. My daughter and my daughter-in-law texted me photos of the bite marks, some taken by themselves and some by concerned daycare workers. My daughters are worried about the biting, but also worried because babies who bite are not allowed to attend daycare. And if that were to happen, my daughters would *lose their fucking minds*.

When I saw the photos, I texted back that it was good to know my grandkids were biting *other* kids, not themselves. I've received no response.

ӭ

My six-year-old granddaughter characterizes my writing *process* this way: She has two pairs of glasses. One for downstairs.

One for upstairs. She mixes them up. She can't wear the downstairs glasses upstairs, or the upstairs glasses downstairs. She pretends to light a candle and puts it beside her coffee cup and then she stares straight ahead at her computer and reaches for her candle. She mimes drinking it, and screams.

Today I looked at pictures on the internet of bodies after being hit by trains. But what I'm really trying to do is research winds for my Wind Museum. I tell myself, Just think about wind. Stick with the wind.

The Saffir–Simpson Hurricane Wind Scale (SSHWS) classifies hurricanes—western hemisphere tropical cyclones that exceed the intensities of tropical depressions and tropical storms—into five categories, distinguished by the intensities of their sustained *winds*.

Now we're getting somewhere.

The skunk with distemper is stuck in the window well again, chewing incessantly on the garden hose that is coiled up in there.

Through my window, across my tiny yard, I can see my four-year-old grandson in my mother's bedroom as he tumbles and jumps and spins. I'm listening to "Le Tango de Chez Nous," and his movement appears choreographed, so beautiful and poetic and playful. My mother is lying in her bed, clapping.

Last night I put this same grandson to bed. I lay down with him in his narrow bed and we talked for a while in the dark, with his head on my shoulder. We held hands. Grandma, he said. Yeah? I said. How old are you? Fifty-eight, I said. And then you'll be sixty, he said. And then you'll be seventy.

And then you'll be eighty. And then you'll be ninety. And then you'll be one hundred. And then you'll be murdered.

What! I said.

I mean and then you'll be dead, he said.

Okay, I answered.

And then I'll wrap you in toilet paper, he said.

Thank you, sweetheartchen.

You're welcome, Grandma.

# Two

April 2023

The Director of the Conversation from the Conversación Comité in Mexico City has written to tell me that my submission is not altogether what they were looking for. The Comité has reiterated that the theme of the Conversación, which will be accompanied by a small book containing the submissions of the participating writers, beautifully illustrated, is: "Why do I write?" My *juvenile* letters to my sister describing a European cycling adventure are not appropriate within that context.

But she is the reason why I'm a writer, I reply. She asked me to write, and I sent her letters. It had never occurred to me before that.

The Comité responds: No, no. The question is not, Why am I a writer, but: Why do I write.

I think: Douchebag question either way. No, no, not douchebag question; douchebag answer. Whatever you do, don't have an answer, period. Also: douchebag to even know the question in the first place.

Prosastuckligeschaft. Prose-stuffed society.

I'll try again. I must get *on* this thing because the Conversación has already been advertised and the dates are set.

If the reason why I write has removed the reason why I write, is it still reasonable to write? (Douchebag or not douchebag.)

∽

February 29, 1996

Dear Marj,
My editor is worried I might be "ennobling" poverty and at the same time he thinks my characters are sometimes jerks, creeps, acting mean, cruel, vituperative, and self-pitying. He says it's impossible to have a woman's name tattooed on your penis and then, when you're aroused, watch the letters grow into a huge reminder of where you're supposed to be sticking your dick. "This is a preposterous plan," he writes.

Meanwhile: I've had an abnormal pap smear. And the Skyline Collection Agency called, only to tell me they're taking me to court over an unpaid phone bill.

∽

When my sister was twelve years old, menstruating for the first time, angry, freaked out and marooned on the toilet, she yelled at me to take money from Dad's dresser and go immediately, hurry, hurry, to Reimer Pharmacy for pads.

Why? I yelled back. What's happening! Are you gonna die!

Don't ask why! Just do it! Go!

Our parents were gone, and it was up to me. I was six.

Soon, I was soaked in sweat, pedalling as fast as I could, balancing a giant box of belted Kotex pads on my bike's handlebars, whispering to myself the words, the battle cry, It's Scooby-Doo or die! I was craning my neck to peer around the giant box, to see where I was going. I was careening off curbs, grazing parked cars, zigzagging from one side of the street to the other, blinded by sweat and pads, and visions of blood pouring out of my sister, and adrenalin and the wild urgency of my mission.

I've never felt so alive, so engaged and determined, so essential, as I did that day, coming to the rescue of my bleeding, dying, enraged (now that she was a woman) sister.

First order of the day. Stop the bleeding.

⁓

After I stood beside the Assiniboine River contemplating suicide years ago, believing that I had destroyed the people I loved most in the world, and managing only to throw my cellphone into the water before being coaxed away from the shore and brought to the Victoria Hospital, the doctor there told me that she'd like to hear my "story." She believed in something called Narrative Therapy. But first we would "do" the Official Comprehensive Psychiatric Evaluation.

In my winter jacket with the torn lining, I sat perfectly still in a tall-backed chair while the doctor swivelled, ever so slightly, from left to right to left to right to left again in her office chair, reminding me of my long-ago boyfriend Wolfie cycling up the steep hills of Northern Ireland. Reminding me of my six-year-old self on the street on my little bike on my life's first great mission.

Was the doctor trying to hypnotize me? Was she feeling agitated?

Here we go, she said. She smiled. Answer as honestly as you can.

Are you having difficulty sleeping?

Are you sleeping more than usual?

Do you wake up in the morning feeling rested?

How interested are you in socializing with friends, family and/or colleagues?

Have you noticed recently that the things that normally make you happy no longer do?

Would you describe your mood as being predominantly dark?

Would you describe your thinking as morbid?

Has there been a time in the last four weeks when ordinary tasks such as showering, answering the phone or preparing food, even a simple meal, required of you Herculean strength?

Have you been unable to stop yourself from crying, or really, well, let's call it weeping, for no reason other than everything?

Do you recall being held in your mother's arms, the sun shining through a patterned curtain—a pattern you can still trace in your mind; in your memory it was full of spirals and abstract doodads, because this was the sixties—on your tiny face, on your soft little arms, on you, your innocence, as you were cradled tenderly by your mother. She sang a lullaby, perhaps Too-ra-loo-ra-loo-ral? *Too-ra-loo-ra-loo-ral, Too-ra-loo-ra-li,*

*Too-ra-loo-ra-loo-ral, hush, now, don't you cry* . . .

In the past, recent or distant, have you experienced a great subversive pleasure in opening all your windows to a sweet, cool spring breeze while keeping your furnace on and pumping warm air into your residence? When that happened, did any person say, "No, no, if you open the windows, you turn off the furnace. That's common sense." But isn't it the scent of the breeze that you want, the way it makes you think, the way it makes you remember? And why should you turn the heat off, why should you have to freeze, when you only want to remember a day when every piece of the puzzle seemed to fall into place? Is that common sense?

Recently, have you been giving away your possessions?

Do you recall sitting second row from the back in Miss Penner's grade one class and noticing she was wearing red-and-white strapped sandals, and you were wearing your Jimmy Walker Dy-no-mite T-shirt, and you raised your hand to ask, "What the hell are we all doing on this planet anyway?"

And some of the kids laughed. And you liked that. But you got in trouble with Miss Penner for saying "hell," and she made you stand between the sinks at the back of the room with your face to the wall. She told you she'd clip your wings, and in that second, she put her hand on your back, on one of your shoulder blades, and you really thought that she knew best. She was your teacher! And you thought that you really did have wings, and that she was just about to clip one off—so you twisted quickly away from her hand, and she called you a lunatic. Were you a lunatic because for a second you thought you had wings? And you wanted to protect them, because why would you have wings if you weren't meant to fly? Or were you a lunatic because you disrupted the class with a few ridiculous words? Just words. Eleven words. They were just words, Miss Penner.

When you hear the word "angel," do you see two boys named Stony and Rocky? Do you remember them liking you (or was it just that you liked them?) and you asked them both to your birthday party, told them there would be angel food cake, and neither one came—one, maybe Stony, had to get allergy shots that day and the other one couldn't come because you were a girl and he was a boy and when you asked what difference that made he said, "Ho-leeee you're a retard."

Do you remember riding your gold bike with the sparkly banana seat and the super-high sissy bar and feeling so free?

## A TRUCE THAT IS NOT PEACE

Do you recall riding around, practising your swearing, practising your whistling, imagining that you were living in California with Kristy McNichol and Jodie Foster and Richard Pryor and the entire Partridge Family, just owning the streets and caring about nothing?

Caring about nothing.

And do you remember Tommy Kornelsen, the teenage boy who played drums in his garage, stopping you in the street and grabbing your handlebars and twisting them and yanking you off the bike? And then he smelled the seat, a big, exaggerated sniff, and smiled and said, "Ahhhhh! Nine-year-old pussy, my favourite." You didn't know what he was doing or saying, and then he took your bike and rode it around pretending to be a girl, saying, "Oooooh, look at me!" And flapping his hands the way he thought girls flapped their hands.

You got your bike back, and your mom said not to be angry because Tommy's dad drank a lot of beer and sometimes chased Tommy around the house with a knife, and you should only forgive him and love him. Do you remember trying so hard to forgive him and love him? You prayed to God to help you, but every time you closed your eyes you imagined Tommy's dad getting drunk and chasing him around the house with the knife and catching him and stabbing him. Stabbing him. Many, many times. Over and over and over.

Do you recall walking home from school, singing, with Adeline and Janine and Rosemary, the cool girls who already shaved their legs with electric razors and wore Great Scott jeans? You sang the lyric "I believe in Malcolm" and they said, "What? What? What did you say? It's 'I believe in *miracles*,' you idiot. Read the liner notes." Do you remember the six and a half blocks you had to walk with them, repeating the words *liner notes* silently to yourself, *liner notes, liner notes*, hiding your shame and red face and self-loathing?

Do you have a sense of unreality?

Can you define common sense?

Do you remember when your cousins came to visit and you had to give them your bedroom, and your sister was forced to share her room with you, and you would pretend to be asleep in the morning while she got dressed, but secretly you were watching her, and you couldn't believe how amazing that was? Watching how she parted her black hair exactly in the middle of her head, and how it hung so straight and shiny, and how she wore an orange men's dress shirt and tucked it just so into her Lee jeans, the ones that had a few drops of paint up on the thigh, her shirt billowing perfectly around her waist, and how she tied her choker in the front so she could see what she was doing in the mirror and then whipped it around super-fast so the knot was in the back and the blue bead was right in the centre of her throat, perfectly in that little hollow? How she grabbed her textbooks nonchalantly as though wisdom was so obviously hers for the taking there was no question that she would grab her textbooks, not gingerly with trepidation, but with such great confidence? *I'm learning all the time*, that gesture seemed to say. *I'm cool and I'm learning all the time, it doesn't even register with me when I grab a textbook from my dresser, I just do it, no big deal, kid, pffff.*

Do you recall any time in your life—or *every* time in your life—when you picked up a textbook, when you tried to make it seem natural and you tried to do it confidently, but you couldn't do it the way your sister did it?

Have you felt ridiculous about the amount of time you spend pondering your relationship with textbooks?

Do you feel inadequate?

Do you intentionally make yourself vulnerable?

Are you haunted by rage and loneliness? By a bone-deep rage?

Do you remember the girl with Down's syndrome in your cabin at summer camp? Do you ask yourself over and over, Why didn't I walk with her, right beside her, when we went to the dining hall? You were marked as "buddies" that day on the schedule, and you walked fast—you knew she had a hard time walking fast, knew she would trip over tree roots when she walked—so she'd be behind you, not beside you. You didn't want to walk beside her. Why did you do that?

Do you remember thinking, Well, if she hadn't asked me to hold her hand we could easily have walked side by side, but she did ask me to hold her hand. Do you think now, All she asked was for you to hold her hand. So she wouldn't trip on the tree roots. Why didn't you hold her hand?

Do you remember her saying, "Would you please hold my hand so I don't trip on the tree roots when we walk to the dining hall for dinner? You're my buddy today, it says on the schedule. Please hold my hand. Would you please hold my hand?"

Why didn't you hold her hand?

Do you remember being a teenager and on a train somewhere in Europe, heading to a big rock concert at that horrible pit in Milton Keynes? There was a guy sitting in the seat across from you and he was dressed all in white and you accidentally bumped his leg with your big black boot, and when you said you were sorry, he said, in a Scottish accent, "No, it's all on me, miss, it's on me." Do you remember how you whispered those words to yourself even when the doctor told you for the hundredth time that you were safe, that you could rest, that nothing was your fault, that you were not to blame?

It's all on me, miss, it's on me.

Do you remember your family gathered around the backyard picnic table eating hamburgers and potato salad in the summer of 1977, the sprinkler squirting around and around and kids playing and screaming "Ollie Ollie Over!"—and your dad is smiling big because you just told him the best joke ever?

"Hey, Dad!"

"Yeah?"

"Did you know that they're planning to change the Golden Boy into a Sterling Lyon?"

Only now do you think, Oh, he might have been fake-laughing for my sake. Because at the time you truly believed that you were a little-girl version of Richard Pryor or Lenny Bruce, you could feel it in your heart, feel the joy—the physical sensation—of making your dad smile. You could hear applause, and the words "a hero's welcome" came into your mind. And you asked your mom, Hey, what's a hero's welcome? and she said, I'm not sure, but we don't have those here.

And do you remember, a few years later, visiting your cool boyfriend at his rooming house in the city? Do you recall how when you knocked on the door to his room, he didn't answer it? He said, Hang on, hang on, don't open that door, and you waited and heard muffled noises before he came to the door and opened it a crack to talk to you, and through that crack you could see legs folded in the bed, naked legs, and then there was a small laughing sound and your boyfriend turned around and put a blanket on the legs? When he turned back and said this wasn't his fault, you thought again, *It's all on me, miss, it's all on me.* And you whispered "Sorry," and the door closed and as you walked down the stairs you said "Sorry, sorry, sorry" with each step until you were at the very bottom. Wow, were you at the bottom.

Do you remember when you were nine years old, and you had North Star runners and homemade blue jeans and a white

T-shirt that felt soft on your body, it was so soft, and the North Star runners fit you perfectly, and you walked through the streets of your town like you were the mayor, like you were the person saving it from drowning, from hunger, from sadness, from everything, and you were free and you were strong and you did this thing you had seen your cool California cousin do at the airport: you tipped your hat in greeting; you imagined that you had a hat, the way your cousin did, and you put your thumb next to your index finger as though you were grabbing the edge of your hat, your imaginary hat, and you tipped it, you tipped it, which meant that you pretended to either pull it down a bit, a quick yank, to say, *Hello, townsperson, top of the morning to you*, or you pretended to lift it right off your head and put it back, and that was more elaborate and you enjoyed doing it and people smiled and nodded and said, Well, hello and greetings to you too, and that made you so goddamn happy?

You tipped your imaginary hat all that day to everyone you met, and they liked it even though the hat wasn't real; they liked the gesture, the old-timey gesture, and they answered it, and you felt as if you were the one in charge and you could save everyone from everything.

What *is* unreality?

Do you experience sleeplessness?

Do you have an appetite?

## A TRUCE THAT IS NOT PEACE

Do you suffer from unrelenting feelings of guilt?

Do you find it difficult to answer your phone? To go out? To socialize? To get out of bed in the morning? To focus on your work?

Hello?

Do you ever think of harming yourself?

Do you have a plan? A considered method?

Do you abuse alcohol or drugs?

Do you have any allergies?

What's your religious affiliation?

Do you have sharp objects on your person?

Do you remember when you were ten years old, and you climbed that tree in the backyard? And the branches were thin but you sat on them anyway and swung your legs, and the branches swayed and you laughed, and you could see for quite a long distance, you could see your church, you could see your school, you could see Debbie's house, you could see the yellow-and-blue fields, and you were wearing your North Star runners, and your mother waved from the kitchen and clapped, and when you came down from the tree the sun was setting and the mosquitoes were coming out and tomatoes were lying on a blanket on the grass and your mom called through the screen, her hand on her chest, and said, Hey, would you mind collecting those tomatoes? Just scoop them up in the blanket like a baby and bring them on in. Just bring them on into the house. Just bring all four corners of that blanket together in your hand and lift it right up and bring it inside. And you were thinking of the number four and the people in your family. And you did just that, lifting all four corners. You had never done that before with a blanket, and you were very methodical about it, one, two, three, four corners together in one small fist, and you airlifted those tomatoes to safety the way you knew people in helicopters let a long rope dangle from the sky and scooped runaway polar bears into blankets and airlifted them back home to the tundra, and your mother was happy and you were so pleased with yourself for understanding her instructions and bringing the four corners of the blanket together that way, expertly, to create a harness for the tomatoes, and you didn't drop a single one, and your mother put her arm around your shoulders and said she was so relieved you hadn't fallen out of the tree.

    And you wondered about that late into the evening because she hadn't seemed worried when you were up in that tree.

    She had seemed more concerned about the tomatoes.

    When you were up in the tree, she laughed and waved and clapped.

    But now you know that she had been holding her breath.

She had her hand on her chest.

She had her hand on her chest.

She was hoping, she was praying, oh my god she was praying, and she was thinking, *C'mon down my love, c'mon down.*

∽

How will it work, my Wind Museum? Will people move from room to room, or gallery to gallery, experiencing different types of wind? How will the wind be made? The different types of wind? How will the wind get into the room? Will there be information in the various galleries—photos, text—or simply the wind? Will we know what type of wind we are experiencing in each gallery? Will there be a gallery where we can experience every type of wind, where all the winds will meet and converge?

I got up very early this morning determined to begin, again, my Mexico City Conversación piece, "Prosastuckligeschaft." But soon I got lost, dreaming of my Wind Museum. I thought of other museums I'd visited. And I thought, Why *not* a Wind Museum?

Other museums and collections I remembered: wax models of eighteenth-century diseased organs in Bologna; artifacts pertaining to heartbreak in Zagreb; the Museum of the Other Woman; museums of pens, resistance, foundlings, torture, brains; and my favourite, with a very long name: *Toto je mile. Mala zbierka cestovnych budikov.*

A *small* collection of *travelling* alarm clocks.

This last museum is in a narrow, crumbling house in Bratislava, Slovakia, a former communist country where it was once largely forbidden to travel. Two old women, the curators, sit behind a rickety table near the entrance, smiling, gesturing, Go in, go in!

"I'll tell you what nice is," they say. "Nice is a small collection of travelling alarm clocks."

Was that a museum of dreams?

The writer Robert Walser told his doctors he was closing his prosastuckligeschaft, he was finished with literary life; they needn't discuss it anymore. And then he spent his last twenty years in a Swiss mental asylum.

Also distracting—in addition to my dreams of museums—is the activity in my mother's bedroom, which is inside the big house that I can see clearly from my little house in the big house's backyard. The "cleaning lady" is standing in the middle of my mother's bedroom, wanting to change my mother's sheets and vacuum and dust, and my youngest grandson, a baby, is bouncing around in there, too, sitting on top of the vacuum cleaner, falling off, getting back on, screaming, pulling books from the bookshelf, screwing up my mother's TV remote control by pushing all the buttons, banging on the head of a ceramic sculpture of a young woman, pushing my mother's panic button, which is glued to her bedside table and sends a shrieking, wailing alarm through the compound, and throwing all of my mother's folded underwear off her bed and onto the floor.

My mother is out of her bed now, and shuffling around after the baby, making whooping sounds of joy that I can hear through her double-paned windows and through my own double-paned windows. Is there such a thing as triple-paned windows? Later, my daughter or son-in-law or E or I, but not really me because I don't understand how to do it, will have to fix her TV and find her remote, which is probably in my mother's housecoat pocket.

Now my daughter, who lives upstairs in the big house, has come into my mother's bedroom and is talking with the cleaning lady, Laura, who is young and French—from Lyon—and "thorough"; and all four of them, my mother, my daughter, my fifteen-month-old grandson, and Laura are laughing. The three women stand in the centre of the room, and the little boy runs from one to the next, darting through their legs, which they spread wide enough to accommodate his small body. Then my daughter takes my mother's hand to steady her, and the cleaning lady picks up the vacuum and the little boy throws himself onto the floor, inconsolable, for some reason.

Do we need a reason?

E wanders into the dining room where I work at the table. I just woke up, he says. I need to sit down.

He tells me he's developing feelings of sympathy for the distempered skunk.

Then he tells me about his wild dream last night: I was in bed, naked, he says, with my ex-girlfriend. She wanted to make love but all I could do was—

I look at him: Why are you telling me this?

All I could do was cry and think of you and how much I missed you and how much I loved you. And only you.

And then what happened? No, don't tell me.

The dream, he explains, is about how much I love you.

And conveniently you can have sex with your naked ex-girlfriend at the same time.

(E, there are dreams we don't talk about. So far this morning you've told me that you love a diseased skunk, in waking life; and you're dreaming of your old girlfriend, in bed and naked, in your subconscious life. Where does that *place* me? As the young critics say.)

⁓

Earlier, my mother left me a cheery message attached to the patio door with a blue rubber band. It's in the form of a bright-yellow postcard from Lutherhaus Eisenach with the quote: "*Man dient Gott auch durch NICHTSTUN . . . ja, durch nichts mehr als durch NICHTSTUN.*"

"One also serves God by doing nothing; indeed, by doing nothing more than by doing nothing."

⁓

*Cleomenes, King of Sparta.* Slashed himself from shins to belly.

*Andrea Dandolo, Venetian admiral.* Beat his head repeatedly against his flagship's mast.

⁓

My sister's old boyfriend has become *the* world expert on The Barrel. Recently, he wrote a treatise entitled "The Casks from La Belle, 1686." Subtitle: "Stowage and Packing Containers." You can read about it in *La Belle: The Archaeology of a Seventeenth-Century Ship of New World Colonization*, pages 291 to 331.

Did my sister have dreams about him, naked and in bed with her, wanting to have sex? Was he one of the good things she may or may not have been thinking about in those thirty seconds of lucidity following death?

I had a recurring dream after my father died, I tell E now. If you want to talk about this sort of thing. In the dream, he is lying battered and bloodied on the tracks in the woods near Marchand, Manitoba, and pleading with me to help him. He isn't speaking but his arms are outstretched, and he is looking at me, begging. I'm in a phone booth. In reality, there is no phone booth near that stretch of tracks. But in my dream, I'm in a phone booth and I'm talking on the phone, I don't know to whom or about what, and I'm trying to gesture to my father, through the glass of the phone booth, to just hang on for a sec, I'm busy, I'm on the phone.

"Nothing accomplished." My father's last words. Or: almost last words.

His *last* last words may have been, "I'm aware of that." Those were his last words to me, anyway. I had driven him back to the hospital in our hometown after our family lunch in the city, where he'd pleased my mother by ordering a ham sandwich, and where he'd discussed colours with my daughter and watched my son disappear from view.

What had he been aware of?

I told him that I had to go. I had to drive to the city, to get back to my kids.

"I'm aware of that."

But wait, no, his very last words to me were, "And I, you."

⁓

"One also serves God by doing nothing; indeed, by doing nothing more than by doing nothing."

And: "Until a man is nothing, God can make nothing out of a man."

That's easy for Martin Luther to say.

⁓

I imagine my sister and me joking about her boyfriend being a world expert on The Barrel, how we would find it unbearably funny while others around us would say, sternly, But barrels—if you only knew their history—were the very implements that saved lives! They represented a new and revolutionary system of preserving food and drink for long sea voyages, without which men would certainly perish or succumb to . . .

And my sister and I would laugh and laugh and laugh and laugh.

Were all girls from Steinbach, Manitoba, taught to despise ourselves *and* our voices?

In one of my more recent dreams, Mel Gibson stole my cellphone. Then someone shot me at close range, in the face. And my mouth flew off down a narrow white corridor. And I was so angry, in that dream, for not getting out of the way of the bullet. I lost my mouth. Who shot me? Did I shoot myself?

Years ago, when I threw my cellphone into the Assiniboine, I had considered also throwing myself into the river. But I managed only to throw my phone. A parable of perfect silence.

Another parable: The first time I was invited to visit another city as a writer, I was housed in the backyard shed of an associate professor at the university where I'd be reading. A different professor, a poet, who'd arranged this trip, was supposed to have picked me up at the train station and housed me. But she had fallen in love. Now she couldn't put me up at her place after all, because of falling in love, and she couldn't pick me up at the station either. Love is love. Poets! The other woman, the associate professor, showed me the shed and said she was sorry, but it was the best she could do. She had moved the garden tools and lawn mower and oily rags into one corner of the shed. "Please don't smoke." A blow-up mattress lay in the other corner, with an air pump beside it in case it deflated during the night, as it was prone to, and the professor had brought in a lamp for me to use but *only after dark*. If you need the washroom, she said, please come to the house but knock first. Her five-year-old daughter was having a birthday party, and the professor was concerned that I would frighten the children if I, a perfect stranger, a perfect smoking stranger, suddenly appeared in the house needing to urinate. Then I learned that my reading was cancelled because the poet, whose class I was supposed to be attending, had left town with her new love. I stayed in the shed for three days, at night waking up every hour on the hour to pump up my bed, or to smoke outside in the dark, or to pee discreetly beneath a tree in the corner of the yard, until my train was scheduled to leave, and I went home.

⁓

Recently, an all-women's university English class in California has, after much consideration, absolved me of guilt for writing one of my books in my father's voice. *Because I did it with compassion.*

"Betray him, Atlas!"

Those are the words I heard one boy say to another (a boy named Atlas) at the playground near my house the other day. The language their game required. I locked eyes for one second with the boy who was about to be betrayed by Atlas and then looked away forever.

Did I do so with compassion?

Or something else.

⁓

After my father killed himself, my mother stopped opening her mail, moved to an apartment in the city a few houses away from mine, and began to memorize three-letter words. I photocopied hundreds and hundreds of pages of three-letter words for her to memorize, and she kept these in piles all over her apartment, in every room, on every surface.

Was writing in the voice of my father an act of compassion? Or born of an urgent need to know why and how, a creative act from a deep, dark hole, a well of fear: Would I do it, too? If I could become my father, I would understand. And if I could understand why and how, I could understand why not and how not.

Literature is not *compassion*; it's war.

Confetti war. Sitzkrieg.

I have no words, my mother said.

But there they were—all the three-letter words we could find. She began hosting Scrabble tournaments in her home. One day, three young men from mainland China showed up at her door. They were travelling around North America, from one Scrabble tournament to another, living in their van. They didn't speak English but they knew many English words, enough to win at Scrabble and make a bit of money to pay for food and gas to get them to the next tournament.

My mother was thrilled. She had heard of these fellows. They had heard about her. They are from mainland China, she said to me in wonder, several times. She got on the phone and arranged a two-day tournament at her place, six games going simultaneously. Sanctioned Scrabble rules. Timers. Twenty minutes of play per player. A purse of five hundred bucks.

In the middle of one game, my mother struggled to breathe. She motioned to her friend Renata to help her find her nitro spray. The bottle was empty. Renata called an ambulance, and as my mother was being wheeled out of the dining room on a gurney she yanked her oxygen mask off and craned her head around to talk to the Chinese men.

Now listen, she said, you stay here and wait for me to get back. There is clean linen in the hall closet.

The paramedics asked my mother not to speak, but she managed to say, There's a frozen chicken in there! She jabbed a finger in the direction of the fridge.

The men didn't understand her words, but they got the message. The tournament was over, my mother was off to the hospital, her friends left; but the three men stayed put, as directed. When I showed up at my mother's place later in the day to pick up some clean underwear and a book and her toothbrush and housecoat, I discovered the men sitting around her dining room table eating chicken soup. I had no idea who they were or what they were doing there. And they weren't able to explain it. I looked around. The kitchen was immaculate, shining. The men had even polished the range hood. They had neatly folded my mother's tea towels and hung them perfectly on the oven handle. We stood around and smiled at each other, desperate for understanding. Finally, one of the men brought out a Scrabble board and showed it to me.

Aha! I understood. The three men conveyed to me, without words, that they were worried about my mother. And I conveyed to them, also without words, that she would be okay, she'd be home the next day, or the next.

A week before this incident my mother had been kidnapped from her house by two Mennonite men who spoke only the old language, Plautdietsch. She was taken to an ATM and told to withdraw all the money from her account and give it to them. These men had been driving around looking for someone to hit up, and when they saw the "Welcome to the Toews Household" sign that my son had made for my mother in his seventh-grade woodworking class, they knew they'd found their mark, one of their own. They'd hoped that she would speak their language, which she did, and does, and they managed to convince her that they needed money. They had many hungry children at home, they said, having recently arrived in Canada from South America, and would she go with them right then and clean out her account?

Luckily, a gas station employee who was stocking shelves next to the ATM was suspicious of the transaction and phoned the police. But before the police could arrive, and before my mom had drained her account, the Mennonite men fled. This must be the first kidnapping and attempted robbery conducted exclusively in Plautdietsch, complete with cooperation and much camaraderie.

⸺

When my father didn't speak for an entire year, the first year of my life, he would walk and walk and walk until his feet bled and his long body collapsed next to my tiny one on the living room floor. He'd look at me and wonder: Who is this?

My sister became a sleepwalker. She would play the piano until her fingers bled and her knuckles swelled, and her head fell onto the keys.

When my sister was ten years old, she was plucked off the street by a group of teenage boys, driven around, messed with, doused with a vile brown liquid, and dropped off again in front of our house. I watched in silence as my mother cleaned my sister, washed her face, her arms, her legs, removed her soiled clothing, wrapped her in a blanket, in many blankets, held her, murmured.

(Did my sister murmur? Was anything said?)

My mother threw my sister's new furry white hat, ruined, into the garbage. For several days afterwards I'd sneak into the kitchen and quietly open the lid of the garbage can and stare at the hat.

It had happened. And now it was in the past.

∽

"But for those who wish to erase their selves by writing: Why write at all?"

—Yiyun Li

"When one does not have to account for one's own existence in it, however, the world offers abundant joy."

—(ditto)

∽

My oldest grandson tells me he loves me.

"And I, you."

This makes him laugh. He tells me to say it properly. Say it right!

Then he tells me he can't go to school today because his teacher is not there.

Where is he? I ask.

He passed out, says my grandson. And then he died.

Meanwhile, my youngest grandson is teaching himself to walk backwards.

⁓

In her late teens my sister went silent for the first time. She didn't talk for months. Had my father taught her this?

Once years later, during one of my sister's great silences, my young daughter sat quietly beside her on the couch, watching cartoons. During the commercials she put her head on my sister's lap and my sister rested her hand on my daughter's small shoulder.

The Aeolian wind is described in the Merriam-Webster dictionary as "giving forth or marked by a moaning or sighing sound or musical tone produced by or as if by the wind" or "borne, deposited, produced, or eroded by the wind."

In the weeks following my father's death I yelled often, viciously, in public—and always at men attempting to explain the rules to me. There were no more rules; every rule lay smashed to pieces on the ground. Don't talk to me about rules. I'll smash your face in with a brick. I. Hate. You. How dare you tell me that my children are not allowed to play pool in this activity room for seniors only? No, they will not rip the felt!

No, they will not destroy your chalk and cues! How dare you tell me that I am not allowed into your fucking pansy-ass theatre because I'm one fucking minute late for the opening curtain. I have a fucking ticket. I have a fucking ticket!

Compassion?

# Three

April 2023
I need to prepare my Conversación piece for the Mexico City conference.

I also need to think about my Wind Museum. What is my organizing principle?

And I need to talk my ex-husband into giving me back some of my royalties.

Sprezzatura: the art that conceals art.

∽

Two lines towards the end of my sister's journal:
"I Kant! I Kant! C'mus! C'mus!"
"Alright, we'll live as if there is a God."

∽

My mother tells me that "Mexico" means "navel of the moon."

She tells me to watch out! Mexico City is a mile and a half up in the sky.

I should be careful not to fall off?

You should be careful not to suffocate, she says. Athletes who compete in Mexico City need to train at that altitude first, or they'll stop breathing.

But I'm not an athlete.

But I'm saying you need to be able to breathe.

My mother's pacemaker had been bothering her lately. But after tumbling out of bed—sustaining some dark bruising—she'd declared that her pacemaker is working better now because of the hard knock it took.

My mother takes my grandson's hand and thumps it against the part of her chest where her pacemaker is installed. Feel that? Hard as rock. Punch it. My grandson gently taps my mother's chest with his little fist. Feel that? my mother says again. Let's take it for a test drive. She grabs her great-grandson and forces him into a two-step. Let's rev it up, kid.

I think of the words written on the wall of the women's washroom in the recreation centre at the park, Trinity Bellwoods, near my home. Read that to me, said my grandson.

Only assholes wanna live forever, I said.

Only assholes wanna live forever? he said.

Later, I saw a guy getting into his car across the street from me wearing a T-shirt that said, Assholes Never Die.

⁓

My ex-husband has agreed to meet me to discuss monetary matters. He says, I'll be in the "north-west quadrant" of Trinity Bellwoods Park.

Why does he say it like that? We never used to talk that way.

I hear my mother's words: "But I'm saying you need to be able to breathe."

In preparation for my Conversación in Mexico, I'm learning Spanish from Duolingo. *Yo soy una mujer. Tu es un hombre. Yo como manzanas. Tu comes manzanas.*

I think: *No puedo respirar. Yo soy una mujer. Yo como . . . no puedo respirar.*

∽

"Had I been more disciplined I would have written nothing and lost nothing."

—Yiyun Li

And: "This tireless drive to write must have something to do with what cannot be told."

—(ditto)

∽

Is silence the disciplined alternative to writing?

A student of English Literature, whose class I recently visited, has suggested that now is the time for me to stand back and listen. I've had a "platform" long enough.

But what then—if I stop writing? I don't want a platform. I am listening. What an awful word! Platform.

Dear Comité, Why do I write? The answer is 42.

After her remark about my platform, the student told me that she and her boyfriend and another couple had recently rented an old stone farmhouse in the countryside.

Where I will be exiled for re-education? I asked her.

There was a pause.

I apologized. I was angry, I said, that I was forced to argue with my ex-husband about our arrangement for my royalties. I am angry, I said, at so many things. Men, really, I said. Or, I don't know. I don't know anything. It's so boring. I'm sorry.

The student nodded, put her hand on my arm, and led me away down a corridor.

I'm sorry, I said again and again. I reminded myself to ask about her thesis.

⁌

There's an element of impulsivity to suicide, a therapist friend told me. We were walking along the edge of the steep bluff that forms a horseshoe around Niagara Falls.

Yes? I said.

I don't believe my father and my sister were impulsive. They spent their lives planning their deaths, living their deaths, almost dying every day, dying almost every day.

And they wrote and wrote and wrote. My mother, on the other hand, doesn't want to write or need to write, and she doesn't worry about being understood or about escaping herself or erasing herself. She understands herself. She reads whodunits to solve problems, but not the problem of herself. She is not a problem to herself. And she is not suicidal.

How does it happen that only she among us doesn't write? Has she done as W. B. Yeats instructed? Does she live by conceiving of life as a tragedy?

I once read a description of Jackson Pollock's paintings as "Genius . . . full of symbols that hinted at a subject but never slipped into narrative."

And I thought: Let's set out the douchebag moments in the text and eliminate them.

Narrative as something dirty, to be avoided—I *understand* this. I understand narrative as failure. Failure *is* the story, but the story itself is also failure. On its own it will always fail to do the thing it sets out to do—which is to tell the truth. (Douchebag!) The story harnesses and neuters and confines and kills. Unless there is a reader or a person listening. Or watching. (Douchebag.)

But for those who wish to erase themselves by writing, why write at all? But for those who wish to erase *themselves* by writing, why *write* at all?

I think of my four-year-old grandson, who is creating a series of paintings entitled *Ghosts in Cages*.

I think of my son on that day decades ago when I'd finally worked up the nerve to explain that his father had taken off to Osaka or Hiroshima or somewhere, who knows where, when my son was a baby. It wasn't my son's fault; it was bewildering, I knew that; it was inexplicable, it was so many things, it hurt, it was hard.

And he asked me, tears in his eyes: Can we not go overboard in the talking department?

Once, much later, when my son's girlfriend asked him if he was ready to go to his in-laws' place for breakfast, he pulled the bedsheets up around his shoulders and told her, Picture this: No.

I think of a filmmaker who, when asked about a certain film he'd made, responded: "I don't know why I made it, but I know how . . . by not looking right into a defined, specific image. I want to show with ambiguity (not riddles), with touch, with all that is peripheral, so the viewer can walk in. Yes, walk into the film and be free."

I think: Communion.

I think of standing in Lisbon beside my daughter, who was five months pregnant with her son, listening to fado sung by a mother and daughter, back and forth, to each other. We don't understand the words, but we know the meaning.

Is writing, life? Is it murderous? A crime? Robbery? A kidnapping? An alternative narrative? An alternative narrative to what? Is it both death and survival? An erasure? Is suicide both death and survival? Is writing a type of suicide? Is silence the reasonable alternative to the alternative of narrative? Which is a crime, which a failure? And what happens next? (Doooooooouchebag.)

Why, I asked my mother, were they silent? Meaning, my father and my sister.

That's easy, she said. (Easy?) It was something they could control.

So, not 42.

My therapist friend—the one who walked with me along the bluff around Niagara Falls—had lost a child to cancer. She hated some of the things people said to her afterwards.

I can't imagine your sorrow. I can't imagine your pain.

Yeah, you fucking can! You can fucking imagine it. Go ahead and fucking try.

My friend told me she'd never felt more alone and sealed off in her coffin of grief than when people told her, even lovingly, even with tender hugs, that they couldn't imagine her sadness.

Try! Stay! Stay with me.

What will happen if I stop writing, I want to ask the student of English Literature.

I must travel to the moon's navel and deliver an answer. Soon.

⁓

The sirocco is a Mediterranean wind that comes from the Sahara and can reach hurricane speeds in North Africa and Southern Europe.

Should I have padded walls installed in the room/gallery of the sirocco wind in my Wind Museum to prevent guests from being tossed in the air and slammed into exposed brick? Will there be lawsuits? Waivers to sign? How do I generate hurricane-level wind in a small room?

I make a list:

Wind Museum.
Deranged skunk.
North-west quadrant with ex.
Conversación in Mexico City.

I add a new item to the list:

Neighbours.

One of our neighbours (but not the one who stalks through the back lane screaming revenge) objects to the backyard house we've built. This neighbour says it will decrease their property value, have an impact on their privacy, and block out their sky.

*And how many people will be living in your house! Do you have a permit for your back deck, for your addition? And how many doors do you have! This is an R1 zone. One residence. One family per house. And why haven't you fixed up your lawn! Why haven't you planted nice things! How many people will be living here!*

E is angry about this, understandably, raving about NIMBYs, about municipal bylaws and city codes. I find it hilarious, a Road Runner cartoon. Soon boxes from Acme Corporation will be delivered to our neighbours' front porch. Soon the neighbour will be lobbing explosive-filled tennis balls into our yard and dropping anvils on us from a second-floor window.

My neighbour summons me to her backyard to talk about our "issues." Although I want to laugh, I attempt to appear serious and grave—my brow furrowed and my lips pursed. My neighbour tells me she isn't "trying to tell me how to feel."

To which I respond, in jest, "not yet"—and she screams, Get out! Get out! Get out!

I say, Are you okay?

No, I am not okay!

Our eyes meet and we hold our gaze for several seconds before I leave, as instructed.

Later I dream that my neighbour's partner comes to my house and tells me everything will work out, that we should try meeting again.

She'll be kind, the partner says in my dream. Don't worry anymore.

⁓

*When we do we really do but we don't really, do we.*

*When we do we really do but we mostly don't, do we.*

I'm trying to decide which of these sentences is best. It's dialogue I overheard on the streetcar. A young couple was talking with each other, and with another young couple, about fighting.

Do you guys fight a lot?

When we do we really do but we don't really, do we?

This is one of the most beautiful arrangements of words I've ever heard.

Here's another overheard arrangement of words: A father and his two kids were waiting for an hour, in a long line in the Southern heat, to ride a giant Ferris wheel, only to have the operator shut the ride down at the precise moment the father and his kids made it to the front.

The father said, slowly, locking eyes with the sullen teen operating the ride: Well, that's dang fine, standing in line, don't get to ride.

The meaning of life, overheard at a tiny carnival in the Ozarks.

⁓

My mother and me, standing at the open coffin of my sister, her head sewn back together, a capital Y in stitches across her face.

Good question.

He'd done his very best. This is what the man who made the stitches told us.

We looked at my sister.

At what point did we look away, at each other, and leave?

I didn't understand my sister's silence. It annoyed me, disturbed me. Do I understand it now? Now that I am older?

I don't want a platform.

My sister is the stark white space around our cluttered, battered, inserted, deleted, ridiculous prose, our messy ink, fouling octopi trapped in barrels on boat decks, gulls shrieking, flailing, dark words and murderous sentences. And she says infinitely more than we do.

In that silence was she holding on to something tightly with every muscle, every bit of energy, her soul, her self? Tethering?

⁓

Earlier today I went to the park to argue with my ex.

I was nervous. I was afraid my argument wouldn't work. I rehearsed what I'd say. I didn't really want to confront my ex; I just wanted all my royalties. Would I force him to an ATM where he could empty his account and hand the royalties over?

I imagined what my ex would say: By leaving, I had destroyed my family. I had killed them. We had made it for so long. We were at the front of the line and then the ride was shut down. By me. I was a monster. Medusa. I had torn their world apart. Like a hurricane wind. I had blocked their sky. I had collapsed their home in on itself.

Now I am back from the park. If I were my elementary schoolteacher father, I'd give myself a C+ on this particular assignment.

My ex and I stood near a picnic table in the north-west quadrant of Trinity Bellwoods Park. We both held takeout cups of hot coffee and did not embrace. My hands shook and my coffee spilled and burned me. I didn't flinch.

My ex wore shiny boots. Nice, I said, and pointed at them. He rolled his eyes.

I told him, Okay, here's the thing. I want you to agree to end this stupid agreement that is unfair because writing is how I make a living and because you have your own salary, and because it's a plan I only agreed to under duress when I wanted everything to stop and because I thought at the time that you were right and I was wrong. I want you to do this and shake on it.

My ex-husband sighed and pondered and sucked on his vape and shifted his weight from one shiny boot to the other. He told me he'd think about it.

You've got one week, I said. I walked away and through each quadrant of the park.

Then I went home. I struggled to breathe. I had wanted to tell him that I was so sorry, so sorry for making him cry and cry, in the car, with his ruined ham sandwich, soaked in tears, in an electrical storm at three in the morning, in the rain, huddled in the yard, comforting our terrified dog, and trying to be comforted in exchange by a dog, a dumb dog, in a storm, with dangerous electrical wind, it was so windy, and that I loved him and I missed him and I was so angry with him and so fucked up and so stressed out and so worried and filled with dread, creeping, shape-shifting dread, and could I just sit next to him, breathing, remembering—just sit very close to him with his arm around my shoulders at that stupid fucking picnic table in the north-west quadrant for just one minute?

Mennonite women wanting to leave their lives have been showing up at my mother's place. They've heard she speaks their language, is one of them, and that the coffee's always on. She's running a safe house now. Angry husbands are shooting at her living room window, putting bounties on her head. She's not afraid. She quotes her father: You can kill me, but you can't scare me.

Now, she tells the women, we have options. Sit here with me and let's discuss.

⇁

"The urge to destroy is also a creative act."
—Bakunin the Anarchist
(and every one of my female friends)

⇁

Why did they do it, my father and my sister? To kill themselves, to stay alive, to stop themselves from moving further and further away from the truth, that aimless drift, that spit of land? Or to escape the truth?

Is writing the acceptable alternative to killing oneself? Does suicide end the pain and preserve the truth? Does writing attempt to achieve the same thing, and are both suicide and writing incomprehensible?

I wouldn't use the word "futile," I once said to my Russian Jungian shrink about writing. But did I say that because I didn't want to be locked up?

Why write?

How I wish the question from the Conversación was simply: Why?

The Y carved into my sister's face, stitched up, answered, emphatically, finished.

What a fucking bullshit thing is this fucking bullshit Conversación I'm supposed to be writing for Mexico City! A mile and a half up in the sky in the navel of the moon. Somebody told me that living in Mexico City is like smoking one and a half packs of cigarettes a day, so I will start smoking now as part of my training for the Conversación.

The deranged skunk is now trying to get into our house every night, clawing and clawing for hours, always in the same place, against the north-facing wall outside my mother's bedroom. We've reinforced the wall with concrete and wire mesh. We've put a small container of wolf urine under the deck (so the grandchildren don't find it and drink it) next to the wall, as recommended by an expert on pest control. How does one acquire wolf urine? We've set up an old clock radio to play the shitty middle-of-the-road rock that skunks hate, and we have shone a bright light on the spot on the wall where the skunk is desperately attempting to break in, to return home. Nothing will stop her.

Many years ago, my children and I watched a tightrope artist perform on the boardwalk in Halifax. He did tricks on the wire. He was a clown. But not a particularly good one. He fell off his wire, even though it was only a foot or two above the ground, and began to moan. He lay there crumpled and clutching his ankle and calling out for help. He took his hat off and put it under his head as a pillow on the hard pavement.

We laughed and clapped. We thought his fall was part of the show, that he'd get up, bow and pass his hat.

But he didn't get up, and he didn't stop calling for help. Nobody in the audience moved to help him. We laughed, then we stopped laughing and looked at him, at each other. What was happening?

I'm really hurt, he said. The show is over.

We didn't believe him. How could this be? He hadn't merely broken the fourth wall, he had broken every rule of show business. Eventually an audience member went to help him, waving the rest of us away. It was true—the wire artist was genuinely injured, and the show was over. My kids and I wandered off, embarrassed and unsettled.

Why did he do that? my daughter asked me. I shook my head. My son looked away.

It haunts me, the memory of the wire-walker's unwillingness to go on with the show.

⁓

Suicides and overdoses are now being called Deaths of Despair in the newspapers, in the studies, in the statistics.

My therapist friend says: We'll be dead, so we won't feel pain, yes. But in the meantime, we *anticipate* the end of life, of love, of beauty, of the beautiful world, and in that anticipation, we feel so much pain that we bring on the end. To end the pain of anticipating the end.

⁓

My ex-husband (and how could that Vegas wedding have been legitimate?) and I meet again in the park, this time in the southernmost quadrant, bordered by tennis courts on one side (there are always courts looming on the sidelines of our lives) and Queen Street on the other. He has agreed to let me keep my royalties—but only if I also sign a new contract stating that I will give him a certain percentage of fees pertaining to any film rights optioned, and films made, from my books—at least, the books I wrote while I was married to him. He has heard that this is where the big money in books is—which is to say, in movies.

My knees are trembling. He isn't wearing his shiny shoes this time. I tell him I'll think about it.

You've got one week, he says, imitating me.

Nice one, I say. Callback.

⁓

An old friend from Winnipeg says to me, Well, now you're a grandma. So what are you doing to keep busy these days? Just going around stirring up shit?

I remember bumping into my kids' old gym teacher years after my kids had become adults. I'm a docent at the terrarium, she said.

Aha! A docent at the terrarium, I said, not understanding what I was saying but wanting to repeat those words forever in my mind.

⁓

A week later my ex-husband and I meet again, this time in the quadrant of the park where we first met when we started this conversation. So? he says.

I'd thought hard about his proposal. No, I answer. I've made a decision. I won't give you anything anymore, none of it, and there isn't much. As you know. Ten years. That's long enough, isn't it? To be punished for leaving you?

We are silent.

Deal? I ask him. Let's shake hands.

I guess I have no choice, he says. We shake on it.

I give him one last cheque for the amount owed to him that year, as per our original deal, and apologize for everything being the way it is. (Oh, how I wish I hadn't broken my grandson's magic wand.)

As in, over? he says. He is annoyed with me.

And then he is gone.

∽

My sister made a decision. She would not give me, us, the world, any more of herself.

She made a choice. "Will you let me go?"

"A lower key of feelings," from Camus's *The Myth of Sisyphus*.

I guess I have no choice.

∽

Once, I acted in a movie. I annoyed that director *tambien*.

Halfway through the shoot, believing I wasn't needed for a few days, I took off for Paris. I came back a week later and chopped off all the hair extensions the director had insisted I have glued onto my head. Why not wear a wig? I reasoned. I laughed at the director when he asked me to take my clothes off, and altogether stopped taking him seriously when he told me, *Debes estar preparada para morir*. I refused to ride alone in the truck with the guy "playing" my husband, which the director had begged me to do to get to know the guy better and create more loving chemistry between the two of us. I told the director to fuck right off when he called me a prude. I refused to cook meals for the crew after the local woman he'd hired was kidnapped by a cartel. I ruined takes by laughing. My breathing was "visible" when I was supposed to be dead. I walked too quickly. I spoke too quickly. I was not friendly with my "husband" off set. I went a little crazy in the desert and asked for books in English. I asked for a pillow. I asked for an extra blanket. I asked for a bed. I asked for the pit bulls to be tied up. I asked for the guns to be left in the truck. I asked for the grass around the tree where I was to crumple to the ground and die to be checked, first, for rattlesnakes. I wasted everybody's time. I wasted expensive film. I tested the director's patience. I was not a professional. I skipped out of the premiere at Cannes and went on a road trip by myself to Montana instead.

And then I turned the whole thing into fiction and the director into a lunatic.

Burn it to the ground.

Or, wait.

Long ago, I was a flood inspector in Winnipeg, Manitoba, a city that floods routinely because it is in a flood valley, the Red River Valley. I wore a headlamp and carried a clipboard and scrambled around on my hands and knees in people's basements and crawl spaces, documenting all the damage the water had wrought on their lives and then, according to some system created by the emergency measures organization of the provincial government, came up with a figure, a dollar amount, of damages to be awarded. Distraught men and women would stand at the top of their basement stairs calling out to me below, Is it bad? Is it very bad? Is everything destroyed?

∽

This week our angry neighbours, whose sky we've blocked and whose yard I was thrown out of, have moved away, left for good without a word, in the middle of the night.

∽

Years ago, after my ex-husband and I split up, my mother took me on a Caribbean Scrabble cruise. My kids had left home by then, for Montreal and New York City. And in Winnipeg, my sister was getting sicker and sicker, not leaving her house, not eating, not speaking. I was crazy with grief, guilt and dread. My legs weren't working properly. They were stiff and foreign to me, wooden spokes that seemed ready to crack or fly off at any moment. Any time I walked it felt like the first time.

My mother understood I needed . . . something. She suggested a Scrabble cruise. There would be a Scrabble tournament on the ship. Many of her friends from around the world would be there. They'd play eight games of Scrabble a day in a large banquet room, and I'd stay in our little cabin high up on the seventh floor and work on the edits of my latest thing. (I'd call it a "manuscript," but I hate that word.)

Before we set sail, we had to rehearse putting on our life jackets and walking without talking (so we could hear evacuation instructions) in a line with the other passengers towards the lifeboats hanging off the sides of the ship. After we left, on port days we'd get off the boat together and roam about on land. When I needed a break from the edits, I would walk around and around the track on the top floor of the ship, listening to music through my headphones, peering off to sea, trying to sort myself out, trying to complete a thought, to get my legs to work, to get my brain to work.

One night I woke up and thought: This boat is really rocking. My glass of water slid to the edge of the nightstand. My mother snored in the twin bed next to mine. I whispered to her, Mom, Mom, MOM. She opened her eyes. I said, Mom, we're really rocking, eh? Well, honey, she said. We're on a boat. She immediately fell back asleep and resumed snoring. In the morning the sea was calm. My mother went off to the banquet room to her tournament. She was doing well so far. She'd won most of her games. She knew her three-letter words. She'd studied them, memorized them. She knew so many words, weird words, not just three-letter words. Words without vowels, words that seemed so unlikely, words that nobody ever, ever used. And it didn't matter what they meant, so long as they were words included in the most recent edition of the Official Scrabble Dictionary. I laid all two hundred pages of my thing out on the beds and on the floor of the cabin, in order, neatly. I walked carefully between the rows of pages and stared at the editorial notes written in the margins. My legs were beginning to work. The balcony doors were open. The sun shone. It was a beautiful day. We were somewhere off the coast of Cartagena. I heard my mother laughing in the corridor with a couple of her Scrabble friends. They were on their lunch break. She opened the door to our cabin and in that instant a mighty wind raced through the room, scooped up all my pages, every single one, and whooshed them through the open balcony doors and out to sea. My mother and I stood at the balcony railing and peered down at them in the water. Cross draft, my mother said. A few of the pages floated serenely on the surface for a minute or two like lily pads, stark white against the darkness, and then sank.

What is a type of wind that changes direction very quickly, in an instant?

A backing wind. Backing winds can change directions at angles of 180 degrees.

Whatever happened to my family's boat from my childhood? Where had it gone? Why were we so happy to be marooned on an uninhabited island? Why were we laughing?

There's an element of impulsivity to suicide.

Trade winds are so named because if you have a ship full of goods to sell or trade, and no way to get it to the place where you want to sell or trade it other than your sailing vessel, a reliable and predictable wind that always blows in the same places in the same direction would—

——I won't have the trade wind in my museum. A reliable and predictable wind? In my museum?

No.

Abrolhos
Alize
Bora
Brickfielder
Calima
Cers
Chinook
Diablo
Etesian
Fohn
Halny
Hamsin
Harmattan
Helm
Levante
Mistral
Monsoon
Pampero
Roaring Forties
Santa Ana
Simoom
Sirocco
Tramontana
Vendaval
Zonda

My son, when he was four, wrote a message on a coaster in a café where he and I and my sister and mother were having lunch. We were busy talking, laughing, exclaiming! We didn't notice when he left the table.

On the coaster, my son wrote: "I have run away for the thrd tim."

How fascinating that he got the complex tense correct when he couldn't spell "third" or "time." How bad a mother I must have been. How bad a wife.

When my son was turning five, I asked him what he wanted for his birthday.

Rope, he said. Nothing but rope.

He got the rope, a lot of it—good, sturdy thick twine, a beautiful circle of bright-yellow rope from Home Hardware—and with it he created a giant web around the house of things tied together, and to each other, kitchen table legs to sofa legs to TV (this made watching the television difficult, peering at the screen through strands of rope) to curtain rods to piano to laundry basket to lamp to stair railing, to newel post. We manoeuvred ourselves around and through the web for weeks and months. Even the dog was forced to two-step, daintily, methodically, her way through the web to get to her water dish, until one day I'd had enough and sat down with my son to talk about his web, the need for it, the possibility that it had served its purpose, that it could be dismantled?

There is a wind called a haboob, not often mentioned. It's in the "disaster" category of winds, a violent and oppressive wind, an intense dust storm that attacks with no warning. How will I incorporate it into my museum?

>   Ali
>   Amy
>   Anna
>   Brenda
>   Carol
>   Christine
>   Claire
>   Debbie
>   Delia
>   Derecho

"No sooner has the ink dried on the page than I'm filled with revulsion."

—Flaubert, paraphrased.

"Life *must* be conceived as a tragedy in order to live it."

—Yeats, paraphrased.

But what if we *don't* conceive of life as a tragedy? Can we live it?

⁌

*Ottilie Assing*. German writer, journalist, feminist and abolitionist. Swallowed potassium cyanide.

⁌

My four-year-old grandson wants my lighter. I want that, he says, pointing to the window ledge in the kitchen.

No, I say. It's a lighter. It's not for kids. It's dangerous.

Is it fire?

Yes.

What is it used for?

To light things.

Like what?

Cigarettes.

My six-year-old granddaughter, visiting from Winnipeg, makes me a pair of wings and tapes them onto my back. I forget they are there and wear them all day, flying to the Metro, to the passport office, to the Shoppers Drug Mart.

My youngest grandchild, now sixteen months old, adds another song to his repertoire. *Knick knack, paddy wack, give the dog a bone*. He doesn't know the words, but he hums loudly for people as we walk the streets of downtown Toronto.

Soon my other grandson will be turning five. I ask him what he wants for his birthday.

A cigarette, he says.

Three years ago, my mother and I travelled back to our hometown of Winnipeg. Actually, Winnipeg isn't exactly our hometown. We come from a Mennonite community about seventy kilometres south of Winnipeg, very close to the American border. Our neighbourhood there is called Hunga Veade, which is a made-up spelling because my parents' language—Plautdietsch, or Mennonite Low German—is a spoken language, not a written one, but in English it means "Hunger Beware." My mother and I had travelled to Winnipeg to see my new granddaughter, her great-granddaughter. In Winnipeg it gets so cold that all the smoke coming from the chimneys of the houses stands straight up, in columns; it can't move or float around like normal smoke. It's as if it were frozen in mid-air. And, when it's that cold, there are these things called sun dogs, two small suns that show up on either side of the big sun. And when you go outside you absolutely cannot stop moving or you'll die. There are two wide, swift-moving rivers that snake through the city, and bridges everywhere, crumbling bridges that resemble dark sutures if you're looking down from an airplane. We rented an apartment near the centre of the city, across the river from the legislative building and a half-hour walk from my son's place, in the West End. There's a seventeen-foot sculpture of a naked man on top of the legislative building, which came from France, many years ago. Everybody calls it the Golden Boy. Twenty years ago, it was removed, for cleaning, and the City of Winnipeg displayed it at a food market downtown so that Winnipeggers could get a close-up look at this giant, gleaming, muscular boy, before he returned to the top of the legislative building.

We were in Winnipeg for two months, my mother and I, to help out with my son's daughters, who at the time were a three-year-old and a newborn. My mother was old, eighty-five, with a bad heart, and all she could really do to help was hold the baby and sing lullabies in her ancient language—which, if you think about it, is a lot. It's almost everything. My mother rocked the baby, which meant that I was the one who ran around all day with the three-year-old. She has silvery-greenish eyes, the three-year-old, and was always brushing imaginary hair out of them, something she started doing when her hair was long, before her mom cut it into a cute bob. We ran and ran. When she got frustrated, she screamed. Long, piercing screams. Her face turned red, and her body shook. When the tantrum was over, it was really over. She was happy again, throwing herself at me and pulling me up from the couch to dance with her like Josephine Baker. She had all these books about famous people, including Josephine Baker. Ask her who wrote *Frankenstein* and she'd tell you Mary Shelley, or who was seven years old when she got her first guitar and she'd tell you Dolly Parton. It was a party trick her parents could play when they had company. She's smart and intense, like her dad. They're both Scorpios, if that means anything to you. Mostly we ran, she and I. It was exhausting but I love her, and, you know, would die for her. That's what grandmothers do, eventually. We make space in the cave for the little ones. We just bow out. Sometimes I'd turn on Netflix Kids and put her in front of the TV with a bowl of mac and cheese—it had to be the seashell-shaped noodles—and I'd go to the hallway and lie down on the floor to rest and feel the cold air that got in through the cracks around the front door.

Most of my time in Winnipeg was spent taking care of my granddaughters and also my mother, who needed help with just about everything, even showering, which was a pretty funny adventure for us both. She had a lot of friends over to the apartment and they'd play Scrabble and drink wine, laughing uproariously, then sighing about things like the brevity of life, then laughing again. I was trying to write a book at the time, but it wasn't going very well, and I didn't really know what I was trying to write about. A line from a book I was reading kept coming back to me: "The air between us crackles, as it does when you speak of your beloved dead." I thought, Yeah, that's right. That's a good way of putting it. A lyric from a song that a friend of mine had written kept knocking around in my head, too: "Forty years of failing to describe a feeling."

When I wasn't taking care of the grandkids or my mother, I'd go walking along the frozen river behind our apartment and I'd think of those two lines, of the air crackling and of failure. I'd walk for miles along the river—we called it the Ass River, short for Assiniboine—trying to nail down a plan for the book I was writing. I had to be careful I didn't walk too far. It was easy to forget about things on the river, to forget that parts of my body were beginning to freeze or that I'd lost feeling in my hands or feet, or that my watery, windblown eyes were almost completely iced shut, and that I needed to get back to my mother. When I got to the apartment, my mother was always still up, sitting at the dining room table, working.

She'd been given a small translating job by a movie producer who wanted to adapt one of my books. She was translating English words and lines into her medieval language, which she describes as *prust*. One evening, as soon as I walked through the front door, she said, Oh, great, hey, listen, I'm having a problem with one of these sentences. The sentence was "I dare you to say no." There was no word for "dare" in her language. I asked her if she could use a word like "defy" or "challenge," and she said, No, no, c'mon, we don't have words like that! She couldn't stop laughing. Really—she almost choked to death. Even as I lay in bed that night, trying to get to sleep, I could hear her start up again with the laughing.

Another evening, I walked for miles on the river, feeling embarrassed about everything, specifically about writing, about being a person who moved words around, trying to make something. I mean, it was all so embarrassing, and it had to do with being a grandmother, a mother, a useless daughter who got exasperated trying to take care of her old mother and was afflicted with this need to write things down. It started when I was a young kid, riding in the back seat of our Ford Custom 500, in the dark, on our way home from the city or from church. There was only one radio station—which I called "the hog-and-crop report"—so as my father drove, hunched over the steering wheel, peering into the darkness, and my mother sat beside him, and I stretched out in the back seat, the radio listed the day's prices on hogs and crops. The list went like this: "alfalfa up" and then some number, "canola down" and then some number, "wheat down" and then some number, "canola down, mustard up, corn up, spring sows down"—it went on and on and, for some reason, my parents seemed intent on hearing the whole thing, everything on the list, and they weren't even farmers.

At about that time, I had taught myself how to touch-type, and while I was lying stretched out in the back seat with the hog-and-crop report droning on in the darkness, I noticed my fingers involuntarily begin to move, but not really, not my real fingers, fingers in my mind, and they were typing every word that was being said. Eventually, the fingers in my mind began to type everything that was being said around me, not just the hog-and-crop report in the car. It would start, first thing in the morning, with my cheerful mother saying, Good morning, sunshine! The fingers in my mind would begin typing, and somehow they kept up with everything that was said, even if I was the one doing the talking. All day my fingers would be typing—at school, while I was playing kick the can with my friends, every shout, every taunt, every bit of conversation, every question, every answer, until I fell asleep, finally, at night, exhausted but happy, or if not happy then relieved, because I had done it. I had typed away the day with the fingers in my mind, as though that were the only way of proving to myself that I was alive, that what I was experiencing was real.

But that wasn't the person I wanted to be anymore as I was walking on the frozen river. I wanted to be a person who would say, smiling, I'm happily retired now, from everything, to be with my grandchildren, to spend time with my old mother, who will die soon . . . Yes, I'm an older woman, a calm woman, I've written enough things, I'm at peace, my days of partying on Milanese rooftops are over, my days of typing every damn thing with the fingers in my mind are over. I'm here to serve, to sit and listen, to comfort, to care for, to encourage . . . not to vent my hideous spleen, not to worry that I might not live much longer, not to rearrange words like a child.

In fact, I have three spleens to vent. My doctor saw the two extra spleens on an ultrasound. It isn't a big deal—the condition is uncommon but not dangerous. My doctor said they were called "accessory spleens." They are like sun dogs seen on the coldest days. And speaking of parts, of body parts: in my original language, in my mother's mother tongue, which is an unwritten language that is dying in the world and that was never very much alive in the first place, the only word they use for "vagina" and "uterus" and "cervix" or "vulva" or "labia" or any of those female parts, is "da mutter," which means "the mother."

One night, I was asleep in the apartment in Winnipeg when a loud snapping sound woke me, and I sat straight up in bed. It was more of a pop, really, like a gunshot. I got up and switched on my dim bedside light and went to the window to see if something was happening on the street. I noticed that the window was cracked—that was what the popping sound had been, the window cracking, apparently from the cold. The window didn't shatter, the shards of glass were held in place, but I knew that I couldn't touch it or open it without the pane disintegrating in my hands. In short, a bloodbath. I went back to sleep.

A few hours later—it was still dark—I was woken up by loud moaning. I ran to the cracked window to have a look.

There was nobody on the street. I heard the moaning again and this time it was louder, and it wasn't really moaning now but words being shouted. The words were muddled and slurred, but they were real words, and they were coming from inside the apartment. I thought maybe my mother had been unable to sleep and had turned on the TV. Maybe she had woken up to watch the curling bonspiel, a tournament in which men and women hurl heavy rocks down sheets of ice and scream *hard, hard, hard.* My mother is almost completely deaf, and the volume would have had to be cranked up for her to hear it. I went into the living room, where she preferred to sleep. The TV wasn't on. There was no bonspiel. My mother was arguing with somebody in her sleep. She was pointing at an imaginary person next to her and—not really shouting but speaking angrily and passionately—jabbing her finger at this person and saying, All the drops of water, all the pieces of soap, it doesn't matter, do you understand! I stood there in the dark living room, listening to her go on like this about other things that didn't matter, jabbing at the imaginary person. She was quite enraged. I wondered if those comments about soap and water were directed at me. After all, I was the one who'd been helping her shower and maybe she had sensed my frustration, although I did my best to hide it. Eventually, she stopped arguing and began to snore and I went back to bed and slept until the sun came up. When I went into the kitchen, I saw that my mother was awake and dressed and playing online Scrabble at the table. I asked her how she was, how she'd slept, and she said she'd had the best sleep of her life! Well, the best in a long time. The next night, and the next, she woke me up again with her shouting and arguing, but now the words were so muffled that I couldn't make them out.

A few weeks later, I was walking along the river again. I had begun to walk at night, after I'd helped bathe the kids and put them to bed and after my mother and I had returned to our apartment and she had gone to bed, in the living room, all tucked in and ready to begin her nighttime shouting. I was trying to organize my thoughts, and everything, every thought, every memory, embarrassed me. I had never experienced such a deep, excruciating sense of embarrassment, of mortification. Was it the embarrassment of wanting to write when I was, by now, a woman in my fifties, a grandmother of four, responsible for the care of her own old mother? I needed my body to turn itself inside out, to expose what was inside and let it blow away and become mist or dust or whatever happens to what's inside a person when her body is turned inside out. I wanted so badly to stop obsessing about rearranging words. I wanted to disappear, or at least I wanted my mind to disappear, to step aside, to stop. I wanted to exist fully as . . . I didn't know what. As a grandmother, perhaps. As a benign but wise grandmother, with a soft lap, a smile, no thoughts but ones of love, encouragement, optimism. No need to rearrange words. And as a better daughter to my old, dying mother, patient, confiding, tender. I felt guilty about everything. I really believed that I had been a terrible mother to my kids, never fully present, as they say, and that the reason for that was that I was always, always a million miles away in my head, rearranging words, long dark sentences on white pages, like the dark, crumbling bridges seen against this snowy city from airplane windows. Maybe I had a soft lap, and a smile on my face, but the truth was I was the opposite of everything I wanted to be. I was so ashamed of being a woman in her fifties who was not the woman she wanted to be. Wasn't that the domain of adolescence? I tried to empty my mind of words. In bed at night, I imagined that my skull was a smooth white shell, empty and glistening. I burned soy-wax candles with soothing scents of grasslands and rain on city pavement. I repeated mantras to myself: relinquish control, relinquish words, relinquish language, there is no such thing as letters, there are no words left in the universe, nothing left to rearrange. I walked and walked, quickly so I wouldn't freeze, and imagined that I was walking away from words, that the words were frozen under the thick ice, that I was stamping them out with my feet as I walked, one after another, creating a vast, icy distance between them and me.

At first, when I started walking on the river, I was almost the only one out there on the ice, especially at night. But soon, it seemed, a lot of people started going there. Some of them were skating, some were hitting a puck along the ice with a hockey stick, some were even cycling, and there was one guy on a unicycle, but mostly they were walking, like me. One afternoon, I ran into a guy I knew when I was about nineteen, and he was almost thirty. He would come to my empty apartment—I couldn't afford furniture—with beer and weed, and we'd sit on my mattress, which was on the floor by the window, and he'd share his theories with me, his philosophy of life. I can't remember what it was. But afterwards we'd make love, and I remember his expertise, if that's the right word, his commitment to the act, my pleasure, his patience, and his, well, his friendliness, really. But now, when we met on the river and I was in my fifties and he was almost seventy, it was a different . . . well, it had a different feel to it. But not entirely. He was talking, again, as though he'd never stopped, about his theories and his philosophy of life. As he rambled on and on, I realized, or at least I thought, that he might be crazy. I don't know exactly why I thought that, and "crazy" was probably the wrong word. But after a minute or two of typical small talk, the kind people make when they haven't seen each other in thirty-five years, he began to talk about his ghosts, the ones who haunted him 24/7, and he began to show me scars from fights he'd been in. It was cold, of course, but he didn't seem to notice. He peeled off layers of clothing to show me the scars. There were a lot of them, and eventually he was standing there on the ice in his jeans and T-shirt, ranting about the ghosts and the cops and feminism and the banks and his mother and, really, the whole world, which had it in for him. As he was ranting, I kept thinking of him and me, by the window in my empty apartment, drinking beer and smoking weed and making love, such amazing love. Finally, I couldn't take it anymore. I was freezing to death out there, listening to him, watching him remove layer after layer of clothing, and I told him I really had to go, but it sure was nice having had a chance to catch up. He nodded, he'd heard me, but he kept talking even as I said goodbye and walked away.

  I continued along the riverbank—people had tied ropes to branches which you could use to pull yourself up to the street—and kept walking. Soon I was walking on the city streets, not the river path—and I realized that I wasn't feeling cold. I wondered if it was because my body had frozen, during the time I'd spent standing still and listening to my deranged but amazing old lover talk to me as he removed his clothing, and maybe I had lost all sensation, all feeling, and would soon be dead, and, if that was the case, I thought, I'd better hurry.

 I walked down Corydon Avenue, up Stafford, to Jessie Avenue, and it occurred to me that I was still alive. In fact, I was feeling warm. I even took off my mitts and toque and stuffed them into my backpack. I wondered if I was having a hot flash—menopause goes on forever—but, really, it was a different kind of warmth, an ordinary warmth, maybe what they call room-temperature warmth. I turned onto Jessie Avenue and walked past St. Ignatius church and past the cranky old woman's house, past the poet's house, and then I stopped and stood in front of my old house, the house where my other ex (not the biological father of my son, who wrote the letter to my father, but the ex who is the adoptive father of my son and the biological father of my daughter, and also the father of a different woman's daughter) and I had lived for twenty years, give or take, and brought up our kids. We had what used to be called a "blended family." That's a nice term for it. I stood on the sidewalk and stared at the house. It looked the same as always, except now it was blue instead of red. The front steps were still crumbling, and still nobody had bothered to build a handrail for the stairs. I kept walking. I turned onto Harrow Street and walked south toward Grant Avenue.

 I was feeling so warm. It was strange. I didn't want to continue in the direction I was headed but I couldn't stop myself. It must have been at least thirty below zero if you factor in the wind chill. I remember telling myself to go back to the apartment where my mother was waiting for me to make dinner or back to my son's place, where my granddaughter was waiting for me to play with her, but I kept walking, I couldn't stop myself, south on Harrow Street and then west on Grant Avenue, past the ugly apartment block where I lived for a year when I was a kid and my father was studying at the university in the city and my sister was attacked by that carful of young men who threw some rancid brown liquid all over her before dropping her back off at the apartment, past the bookstore where I used to work, where I was always late for my shift, past the Petro-Canada station and Grant Park High School, past the huge pool where I sometimes took my kids swimming, and then west to Waverley, south to Taylor Avenue, and then west to the Reh-Fit Centre—where my father was supposed to go after his heart attack, but he refused to wear one of the program's stupid T-shirts and dropped out—and then to the private tennis club next door, where, strangely, my sister arrived, in a cab, ten years earlier, moments before she died. Behind the private tennis club ran the train tracks that she walked toward, after getting out of the cab, and where she then waited—we're always waiting for one thing or another—for a train to show up.

Later, when I returned to the apartment, I realized that I had walked all the way back through the city streets and not along the river path, as I normally would have done. I went to my cracked bedroom window and looked out at the frozen river and at the legislative building and at the seventeen-foot Golden Boy, perched on the very top of the copper dome, one leg raised as though he were in the act of jumping or flying, and I thought about racing down all eight flights of stairs from the apartment and out to the parking lot and down the riverbank and across the frozen path and up the other riverbank—the left bank, you could call it—toward the legislative building, and to the other side of it, where giant bison sculptures guard the entrance, and putting my arms out to catch that Golden Boy as he fell, which he would surely do.

I leaned closer to the window for a better look, my forehead was almost resting against the pane, and it was then that I heard a thunderous sound, a type of explosion, coming from the river path, and I realized that the path was cracking up, that it was the time of the spring breakup, as we called it, and that giant walls of ice, sheets of ice, sometimes more than a hundred feet long and two or three feet thick, were cracking apart and hurtling along on the powerful current of the Ass River, towards the bridges, towards who knows where—the sea, I guess, ultimately. And, just as I began to understand what was happening, the broken window that I'd been leaning my forehead against for a closer look shattered and most of the pieces of glass fell out and down to the street, eight storeys below, except for one of them, which lodged itself deep in my forehead, near my eyebrow, and in a second my vision was obscured, as they say, by my own blood. I think I swore loudly or moaned or something, the kind of thing you do when you're hurt and surprised, and my mother actually heard me, even from the other room, even though she's almost entirely deaf, and came running—well, not running, she couldn't run—she came shuffling to my room and saw me, bleeding, by the window, which wasn't a window anymore but a wide-open square. The wind was coming through, ruffling my hair, ruffling the curtains, the river outside was loud, screaming really, it was all a bit terrifying, and she put her arms around me and pulled me away from the window. She seemed unnaturally strong in that moment, her grip on my arms was almost painful, and she pulled me away and out of the bedroom and kicked the door closed behind her. I remember distinctly how she did that, so elegantly, so decisively; it was so unlikely, she was so old and could barely move, but somehow she managed, even while she was in motion, even while she was holding on to me and pulling me away from danger, to close that door so beautifully. It was very cool how she did it, kicking it closed behind her, moving forward at the same time, oh, I don't know. I'll just never forget it.

# Four

April 2023

The Director of the Conversación has informed me that my submission is still not suitable.

"Please you must simply answer the question: Why Do I Write? What is your reason?"

∽

November 19, 1996

Dear Marj,

My book is at the printer's. We'll have a big party to celebrate it on Friday, December 13. I hope it's fun, maybe even lucky. I'm really afraid—there, I've said it. I'm afraid of how people will react to the book, afraid of nobody liking it, afraid of what Dad will think . . . if he reads it. I want him to know it's a message of love to him, but will he read it? Will he understand it? I wish I could leave town for a few months like Coach Cal Murphy till it's all over and done with. I hope the book doesn't die too quickly on the shelves. I have to prepare myself for that. I have a strange anti-climactic, disappointed feeling. All I want to do is get back to work on the next thing.

I feel like I have to think of new ideas—not necessarily good or feasible ones—for the next book before I'm finished the last one, like I'm stocking up on my prescription before it runs out.

I think I'm nuts. I honestly think I need a psychiatrist or something to help me calm down, to breathe easy, to stop rushing and panicking. Or maybe I just need to drink less coffee.

Thank god Jules gave me this book on panic attacks, and how to stop them—panic attacks are what I get, I know it. Adrenalin, irrational fear—my breathing gets out of whack, my heart races—it's ridiculous. But don't worry. I'm fine. I'll read this book. At first I didn't want to read it because I thought reading about panic attacks would make me have one. But it doesn't. It calms me down to know that there's stuff I can do, and that there's nothing wrong with me. Even though I keep thinking that I'm not getting enough oxygen to my brain and I'm gonna get too stupid to write—and then I'll no longer have my useful outlet and I'll go INSANE! Okay, I'm going to end this letter here. I'm off to shoot pool with Renee. (And some nimrod she picked up at the King's Head who back in 1981 chucked a plastic piss-filled bottle at Billy Bragg's head for being too earnest.)

⁓

Okay, Conversación Director. The writing *is* the reason.

And 42.

Has the reason *I* write been removed by the *reason* I write, even though the reasons *for writing* remain?

When we do we really do, but we don't really, do we?

*I understand entirely*, I write back to the Director of the Conversación.

I am an annoyance. *Soy molesto.*

I annoy myself.

I am a docent at the terrarium.

That is a calming sitz bath of a sentence.

⁓

The Gloombadeeboombadee Literary Prize, funded by banks, frackers, deep-sea mining venture money and the NRA, writes to ask if I'll attend this year's gala award ceremony.

*Lo siento, señores y señoras.* Unable to be there. Will be on a ninety-day worldwide hot-air ballooning adventure.

I go for a walk with my youngest grandson. I keep quiet as he sings, remaining invisible, pushing his stroller from behind. He needs to believe he's alone, independent, somehow magically propelling himself along in the world, a little song-and-dance man peddling his wares in the city. If I accidentally make a sound, or even quietly attempt to sing along with him, he instantly stops, realizes he's not alone, turns and glares at me, then begins to sob.

Is he enraged or relieved?

My mother phones from the hospital where she underwent a stress test. She tells me that during the procedure her blood pressure dropped dangerously.

Oh no! I say.

She tells me that the doctor took one look at her and asked, How are you?

Well, I'll tell you, she said to the doctor. Not great! I'm going out. Goodbye!

My mother and I laugh and laugh.

What did they do then? I ask her.

Oh, they injected coffee into my vein, and I was instantly revived. And then they gave me a ham sandwich.

~

*Mary A. Anderson.* An unidentified woman using an alias. Cyanide poisoning.

~

Two days after my father killed himself, I woke up in the middle of the night convinced that I was dying. I quietly got out of bed, not wanting to wake my husband or kids, or to worry them after everything that had already happened. Talk about overkill.

It was a warm night, unseasonably warm. I drove to the hospital and walked into the emergency room. Through the hole in the glass that separated me from the nurse I whispered, Hello, I think I'm dying.

I was embarrassed as I did this. There were many people with obvious afflictions sitting in the waiting area.

But you're so young, said the nurse. And you appear to be healthy?

Yes, but, I said. I wished she'd keep her voice down.

The doctor and the nurse were quite sure I was having a panic attack, which I think did feel reassuring, although I'm not sure now, looking back, if reassured was *exactly* how I felt. In any case, the doctor said, we'll do tests.

I told the doctor no, it was fine. It was a panic attack, definitely. I'm young and healthy.

I looked at the clock on the wall. The sun was coming up. I had to get home before anyone woke and discovered I was gone.

∽

I've had that fucking dream again! The one about the long corridor, and my mouth being shot off, and my anger at not getting out of the way fast enough.

But this time, in my dream, there was a door. Perhaps it leads somewhere. Or perhaps it was a dream within the dream.

What will I name my Wind Museum? Just "Wind Museum"? Is that catchy enough?

Or: The Winds of the World. International Wind Headquarters. All the Winds of the World, Under One Roof!

∽

At the age of twenty-four my sister left university, left her boyfriend, left the city and moved back home with my parents. She stayed in her old bedroom most of the time, making lists, reading poetry, sleeping, wearing a green terry cloth housecoat, her wild hair a black tornado, her green eyes getting wider and wider, it seemed to me, while she whispered with my mother, late into the night.

Then she stopped making sounds altogether. She wrote words that she sent to me on yellow lined paper, her neat sentences straight at first, then dipping downwards at the end like rigid fishing rods with baited lines.

I was preparing for a trip, I answered back. Yes, I'll write. You live. And I'll write.

She drew a happy face on the page, and one word: *Deal*.

∽

Poste restante<br>1982

Dear M,
We have *panniers* on our bikes, did I tell you that already? I call them saddlebags. Wolfie made them out of sawed-up milk cartons and burlap feed sacks from Frank and Harold's farm. We have Lark cigarettes, patchouli oil, berets and dark shades. We have sketchbooks and variously numbered charcoal pencils. Wolfie has Henry Miller books, *Sexus, Nexus . . . Texas? The Rosy Crucifixion*. I have birth control pills. Did I tell you that when I was getting my wisdom teeth out before this trip, the nurse asked me if I was on any medication and I was going to lie and say no, but then I worried that if I was on medication and they didn't know, they might give me some drug that would combine with what I was already taking and kill me, so I told them I was on the

pill. I just whispered it because Mom was there with me and I was thinking, Oh fuck, here we go; but she laughed and said, Oh praise the lord, that's a bullet dodged. Wolfie and I have five records between us, stolen from you and Wolfie's brother Gus, your nemesis. They fit perfectly into our homemade panniers. Wolfie has *Monk's Dream* and *Exodus* and I have *Broken English*, *Blue* and *Stateless*. We're planning to become artists. Or revolutionaries. Or both. Those are Wolfie's plans. I don't have any plans. We don't have any place to play our records (and we don't have a revolution) but we like having them in the panniers. This is the last time I'm writing or saying the word "panniers." I hate that word. And sorry for stealing your records, but I had to.

Last night two Belfast teenagers and a British soldier were blown to pieces by a pipe bomb planted in a garbage bin by the INLA, an offshoot of the IRA. We saw the awful photos in an old guy's newspaper in a coffee shop. There was music playing in that coffee shop. (Wolfie says to call it a café.) The needle was skipping on the record player and the same song kept playing over and over. *Catch a falling star and put it in your pocket, save it for a rainy day.* Meanwhile, we were looking at all those gruesome black-and-white photos. I told Wolfie I didn't want to be a revolutionary anymore and I could tell he was pissed off about that. He said I was fickle, which just made me laugh because . . . that word. I said, Okay, but better to be alive and fickle than dead and . . . ? Stalwart? Also a funny word. Would you rather be described as fickle or stalwart?

We've been sleeping in cemeteries, in the rain, and our map has disintegrated. We wanted to go to Derry (they— Irish people—told us not to call it Londonderry), to pass by the Maze prison where our hero Bobby Sands starved himself to death, but the rain destroyed our map, and we went the wrong way. Now we just make I Ching–type decisions about what direction to take. And about everything. When we ask people for directions, we can't understand what they're telling us. They wonder what the fuck we're doing in Northern Ireland at this moment in time. I'm beginning to wonder that myself. Anyway, we're rethinking this whole revolutionary thing. I think we'll just be sympathizers, not actual soldiers. Wolfie was like, What about Yeats? So we've made the switch from armed resistance to art. (This also means we can sleep in later in the mornings.) All this to say we've only been here for two days, but we've already made a couple of important decisions—including the decision that we're never going to be offended by anything. And we're not going to be boring or embarrassed. Or squabble endlessly about stupid things. We're going to seek out experiences from now on, and we agree that one set of things we need to experience is physical suffering, mental anguish, and total rejection from the establishment. I don't really even know what the establishment is—but maybe that's because I've already succeeded in being rejected from it. Like, from birth or whatever. So I can cross that off my list. Which Wolfie likes to call a ledger. I can't stand that because first of all it's a money term, right, like for banks? And just because, why? When "list" is already the word?

Wolfie's taught me how to zigzag up hills on my bike. He showed me by meticulously going horizontally across the hill and then back again and then horizontally across again and back, etc. I went so slowly. I was afraid of falling off my bike and rolling all the way to the bottom of the hill, so I started walking my bike up the really steep parts. Which annoyed Wolfie. He said it looks bad and he doesn't like it. He said all men hate it when girls walk their bikes up hills. Meanwhile, I've learned how to blow smoke rings and Wolfie is still trying to get the hang of it.

Our most recent fight is Song versus Book. I wanted to go to Galway after Sligo (pronounced "Slago"), which is where Yeats is buried—well, a bit outside of Sligo in a church yard *under bare Ben Bulben's head*, which is another line from the poem that Wolfie read to me from his giant Yeats book right before I wet my pants laughing and he told me to fuck off. I wanted to go to Galway because of the song "Galway Bay" that you and I sing all the time. Wolfie said, You want to go to Galway because of a song? He wanted to go straight from Sligo to Dublin to see the Book of Kells, which is his soul's dream (what is a "soul's dream"?). And I said, Okay, well, you want to go to Dublin because of a book? How is that a better reason? He said it wasn't a book, it was a medieval manuscript.

Believe it or not, the song won! Which I think happened because, after that Yeats stuff, I agreed to make love with Wolfie on a low stone wall in some farmer's field. Which only happened because he thought the *bucolic setting* was very romantic and wanted to have that memory. The memory of making love on a low stone wall in an Irish field. We argued a bit about the words "making love" because I wish he'd rather just say "fuck." Making love is so stupid, it sounds like baby talk, but he thinks fuck is crude, a word for women he doesn't love or whatever. Obviously then I had to say I loved him, too. And also: *which* women he didn't love? He didn't want to tell me anything about the other women he didn't love and only fucked, but now I'm worried. And I told him what you said, which was that Ted Hughes killed Sylvia Plath, like, not literally, but . . . and that made him mad too. But the fucking on the stone wall—which was really painful, and I still have tiny pieces of rock ground bucolically into my back and ass—combined with the fact that he basically told me there were other women in his life and then saw how that made me feel, allowed me to get my way and go to Galway before Dublin. And this is all because of you, and our song.

We sat on Yeats's grave and Wolfie taught me how to say "Horseman, pass by." He said it isn't Horse *Man*, as in half-horse, half-man, but Horse*min*, as in: guy who rides a horse. Remember Horse Badorties? Dorkydorkydorky-dorkydorkydorkydorkydorky—pages and pages of that? I love it. It's so stupid. Is that book still in your yellow shelf? Right there beside your bed? I bet you could reach out and grab it right now and read dorkydorkydorky for half an hour before you fall asleep. I asked Wolfie if he found it funny that Yeats was imploring us from the grave to leave and yet we were just lying around on top of him all afternoon. Wolfie told me that what Yeats wrote wasn't literal. He meant we weren't supposed to get emotionally involved with life or death—as in we were supposed to cast a cold eye on it. Wolfie asked if I wanted him to read some of Yeats's poetry to me, and I made a grave error (get it?), and said no. I'd rather have him read dorkydorkydorkydorky to me for twelve pages as a kind of endurance test, like zigzagging up hills on my bike, except way funnier and cooler. Which offended him in spite of his vow with me not to ever be offended, and I had to *cajole* him and say, Actually yeah, say your poem, say your poem. To which he responded ". . . *say* your poem? Like, are you five?" So then he said his poem, which was: *Michael Angelo left a proof, On the Sistine Chapel roof, Where but half-awakened Adam, Can disturb globe-trotting Madam, Till her bowels are in heat* . . . etc. I tried very, *very* hard, so hard (I thought of all the terrible things, death and piles of bodies and famine and everything) not to laugh, but I couldn't stop myself from exploding, like from every single orifice, and Wolfie told me to go fuck myself. I got up and walked over to a clump of trees and sat down next to some ordinary person's grave while Wolfie stayed with his beloved Yeats and ate the last of the Nutella. And I smoked the last of the cigarettes, one after another, in silence, blowing smoke rings that he still hasn't figured out how to make.

I just found the card Mom snuck into my saddlebag. It has a picture of two bikes leaning against a wall and a red heart encircling them. She quoted a Bible verse from Isaiah, who was on acid when he wrote it. It's chapter 55, verse 12, the one that goes: "For ye (that's me) shall go out with joy and be led forth with peace; the mountains and the hills shall break forth before you into singing, and all the trees of the field shall clap their hands." And then under the verse she wrote: "I will imagine you, with joy, in peace and beauty. Love, Mom." Please don't burst her bubble by telling her all this stuff about me and Wolfie, I implore ye.

We tried to see the moon rise over Claddagh, which is pronounced "Cladduck," a little fishing village next to Galway, but clouds obscured the moon, and for whatever reason I took this as a message from you, maybe because you said before I left that you and I would see the same moon even though we were so far apart. And then it began to rain, and we ended up spending most of the night in a bar with university students, singing revolutionary songs (Wolfie said they must be revolutionary songs, but we didn't really know) and drinking Smithwick's beer, which is pronounced "Smithicks"—something I learned the hard way. Wolfie told me a guy in the bar was really hot and so handsome with his black hair and pale skin and blue eyes and excellent jeans and long Irish fingers, and that if the guy asked him to go to bed with him, he would. I can't stand the way he says that. "Go to bed." Also, do you think W's gay? He was like, Who cares if he's a guy, heterosexuality is a trap. Desire is desire, right? I've never heard desire being described that way before. But I couldn't be offended or boring, obviously (our pact), so I was like, Well, so would I . . . fuck him. Then W got pissed off and jealous and mad that I'd said fuck again instead of his baby talk for sex. We left the bar and wandered around the rest of the night until the sun came up. We both kept vomiting small amounts—we had barely any food in our stomachs—and discussing the importance of positivity and of the validation of each other's ideas. W said, We will say yes. Always yes. Apparently, that's how collaboration works in avant-garde theatre (according to W). We're almost out of money, we have no food left for breakfast, or any meal for that matter—not that we're really eating *meals,* which is a bourgeois concept according to you know who— or any place to stay in Dublin tonight, but we've agreed (miracle) that the first order of the day, as Mom would say, is to find somebody to take my pants and make them skin-tight, especially around my calves and ankles. And I have to get a pair of black Patrick football shoes. W has to get a pipe and a pair of thick, black-framed glasses and grow a scruffy beard and wear his cycling hat backwards. If we can get all that done, life will be a breeze and we'll never walk alone.

So: the Book of Kells is a treasure of the Western world and the pinnacle of illuminated illustration. For your information. I made the mistake of not staring at it in awe long enough, and also of yawning, and then W started reciting poetry at me: *the only people for me are the mad ones, the ones who are mad to live, mad to talk, mad to be saved, desirous of everything at the same time, the ones who never yawn or say a commonplace thing, but burn, burn, burn like fabulous yellow roman candles exploding like spiders across the stars and in the middle you see the blue centerlight pop and everybody goes, "Awww!"* I was like, Oh wow, you memorized that whole thing to someday use it as an indictment of me? We were yelling—or, he was yelling—and the security guard of the treasures of the Western world cast a cold eye on us and told us to fuck off on our way. Our way to where? Outside I told W I was leaving, going for a walk. Have fun burning like a roman candle, I told him, I'm going to make a collect call home. I'm starving. I don't think I can be a real poet or a revolutionary or a real anything. I can't draw. I hate suffering. I don't want to smear my own shit on a jail wall. I don't even know what a political prisoner is.

I miss you. I miss Mom. I miss bush parties.

Wolfie and I have made up. We promised to remember our pact never to be offended, never to be bored, always to say yes—and we've resolved to stick to it from now on. We had sex on the floor of the engine room of the ferry from Dublin to Liverpool. Your records are still safe! We take them out of the saddlebags and carry them around with us when we're walking in case our bikes get stolen or rained on. When we were having sex in the engine room, I leaned *Stateless* and *Blue* up against the wall right beside me so that I could stare at Joni Mitchell's sad, blue face with her eyes closed, six inches away from mine. It felt like heat was coming off her face. I could have moved just a tiny bit and kissed her.

Wolfie and I fought in Liverpool! I wanted to go to the Cavern so badly, but Wolfie said he didn't want to do the Beatles thing in Liverpool because it was too predictable.

And because it was the Beatles, which he says is "Engelbert Humperdinck music." I said it was not, and anyhow that's what John Lennon said about Paul's solo music, so it's not even an original thing for you to say. And he was like, Oh, you're calling him just *Paul* now? Like the Bible? Just Paul? And I said, It'll just take a minute to see the Cavern. And he said, It's not about the amount of time it would take, that's not the point. So I said I'd go in alone and he said that was pathetic. And I said I didn't mind and while I was in there he could just wait outside and set himself on fire, like in protest. If he has such strong convictions, right, he should just burn for them. Right? Burn, burn, burn! He was about to tell me to fuck off again, but I said, You have to say yes! We made a pact!

⁔

October 27, 1982

(Birthdates of Dylan Thomas and Sylvia Plath. Dyl and Syl. Would they have made a good couple? What is a good couple?)

We're in a youth hostel in London next to St. Paul McCartney's Cathedral. I'm worried that Wolfie is going to break up with me. I have stress zits around the corners of my mouth, dropping into red patches on the sides of my chin. Wolfie has gone off to play his new Irish pennywhistle in Covent Garden. His plan is to make enough pence to buy us some bread and chocolate and maybe a beer we could share eighty-twenty, as in percent, as in he always hoovers these things before I can drink my fair share of fifty. Which he justifies by saying he's a larger person and also doing the dirty work of busking with his pennywhistle. He calls it dirty work, but he also calls it romantic and says that it "eliminates the middleman," which is an expression that he's now using approximately twice a day. He wanted me to busk with him, which meant standing beside him and dancing groovily or swaying mysteriously and beckoning and pleading with people with my eyes to throw money into Wolfie's navy woollen beret. Or to hold the beret because he doesn't like the way it gets dusty when he puts it on the ground. This request is one of the reasons I'm freaking out about him breaking up with me. I told him there was no fucking way I was going to stand next to him swaying and smiling sadly at people faking being strung out and starving (even though I am starving). I asked him what he was playing on his pennywhistle. Like, are they songs? Because I can't identify them. And he said, Obviously it's not about identification, it's about the emotion, and he asked me if I was an artist or what? I said, No, I'm not a fucking artist but neither are you. And then we had a huge fight in the hostel common area. We were hissing at each other about being an artist or not, about my understanding of the word "scrupulosity" and the lyrics of *Blood on the Tracks*, and just a million stupid things that in his mental relationship *ledger* probably registered as, Fuck this, I'm out.

Do you think he'll break up with me?

Now I'm sitting in the common area of the hostel, worrying. I can feel my face breaking out. It's like bubble wrap.

A girl my age lit her cigarette off mine and started talking to me about famous people who've abandoned their children. She said that's what the hostel reminds her of. I asked her if there were places like that, where famous people can leave their kids, and she said, Yeah, they're called boarding schools. It's a network. Then she said this cool thing, like it was a question. She said, Am I bitter? And then she answered her own question: I'd say I was bitter. That's cool, right? I loved the way she did that, like a short conversation with herself. And then an epic haul off her Lark.

It's really cold in here. Everyone is wearing layers and layers and blowing on their hands. Some people have taken the blankets off their bunks and draped them around their shoulders. The common area is filled with comfy couches and cushions and funky lamps with flickering lightbulbs that are burning out, and there are a few long wooden tables that have names and hearts and graffiti carved into every square inch of them. One guy has a boombox and he's playing, really cranked, a Dead Kennedys song called "Nazi Punks Fuck Off." You'd love this song. When this guy started playing it, I thought, Oh, you can say funny things with a lot of energy and really make people mad and happy. Everyone in the hostel went nuts dancing and jumping and slamming and screaming along to the music. It was super-fast, the way the singer said nazipunksnazipunksnazipunksfuckoff! I mean, just try to say it as fast as you can. I just felt very calm for the first time in a long time, hearing this song. And normal. And happy and sort of excited about the future. It's hard to describe. I felt like I was nothing—not an artist or a cool girlfriend or a revolutionary or whatever. I was just nothing. It felt so good. Like a fresh start. Or, not even a start to anything. Anyway, I know I'm not making sense.

Wolfie has come back to the hostel with frozen buns. The boombox guy has left and everyone is lying around again, smoking, shivering, carving shit into the table. I told Wolfie that Lord Byron had abandoned his kid in some orphanage so that he could go party permanently in Venice, that Byron even went to the exorbitant lengths of calling her Allegra, and then just fucked off, as per. Wolfie said, As per what? Why are you always saying "as per" now? I told him I wasn't and that he was always saying "eliminate the middleman." And also "in the arena of." I told him that Einstein had also abandoned his schizophrenic son in Berlin during the war so that he could flee to safety in America. Wolfie told me he didn't even know what I was saying. Did I think children were annoying? Aren't you on the pill? I said, Just imagine little Allegra calling after her father, Byron, Byron! And Wolfie said, Wouldn't she call him Dad? Then I told Wolfie we should go to Greece where it was warm and we could swim, and he said no, he wants to go to Oxford. What the fuck is that, I said, a farm or something? And then he mimed killing himself. He said, Oh my god, like he couldn't believe I was that stupid. I stared at him for a long time, mentally putting a curse on him that his dick would fall off or get snapped off in a bus door so it would happen in public. And then I said, Am I bitter? And he was quiet, totally defeated by his imbecile girlfriend, and I took a long drag off my Lark and lifted my face to the rafters and exhaled slowly and said, Oh, I'd say I'm bitter. Wolfie was so mad he *went drinking*. Which is weird because he didn't make any money from his pennywhistle, so who's paying for his drinking?

A Cypriot actor/dishwasher in training just gave me a sip of his Wild Turkey. Before he left, Wolfie said, Okay, sit here and fumigate, I don't give a fuck. I asked him if he meant ruminate or fume? He said, Fuck you, fuck you, fuck you. Now two American Druids from some place called White Plains are sitting here and talking about hygiene. The older girl is saying the vagina is a biosphere. Like, it's self-cleaning. Just leave it alone, she said. Then for some stupid reason I started talking about Mom and how she'd once told me all of my clothing is self-cleaning because she hates doing laundry. So I guess the vagina is the same? The Druid said, Um, yeah, exactly. It's just a delicate kind of very tough eco-area with its own laws, flora, fauna, mists, and we should just protect our vaginas and leave them alone. I said, Yeah, like the museum of living grasses in Saskatchewan— stay off them and keep to the path. And the younger Druid said, Yeah! Like when you walk carefully around the geysers in Yellowstone. And the older one said, Yeah! Just let it be! And the younger Druid said, Word! Just think of the Beatles song when you feel like digging around or cleaning in there. Just let it be.

*October 30 (?) 1982*

Wolfie and I were lying on our backs in a cemetery that feels like it's about to disappear into the overgrowth. Wolfie said something interesting! "When countries are so old the dead are eventually forgotten, and nobody exists to tidy up around their graves." I've been trying to think of other similar sentences, but I can't. Our map is useless now. It's wet and soft and torn and crumbling away. Wolfie has laid it out on a grave and is trying to figure out where the Thames is, because that is what will take us to Oxford. (If we were in a boat, I mean, because the Thames is a river.) This is what we own right now: Two charcoal pencils. Twelve pounds. Wolfie just asked me if I can draw caricatures for money. I don't know what those are, so I squinted my eyes and looked up and said, Ohhhh, that's an interesting idea. (You know: the way Grace always talks to her kids.) Then I asked W if he had ever wanted to be a head boy, just to change the subject and because a girl at the hostel had told me she'd been a head girl. I was testing W, because I thought there's no way he could know what a head boy is. But he said, No, why would I? I told him I'd met a kid who'd been a head girl. So I'm just asking, I said, and he said he wasn't into that—as if it was a question about music he liked or something.

I'm so homesick. I keep saying *nazipunksfuckoff* really fast in my head, and this makes me feel a bit better. Remember when Grace's kid asked Mom, When you're dead is it forever? And Mom said, You get the picture, boy.

I just love that line.

I'm trying to write something, as per your assignment,

hahaha. Wolfie was like, What are you doing? And I said, I'm friggin writing something down, bro, what does it look like? He asked me what I was writing—I was writing on the cover of *Blue* and I told him it was a dialogue, a short one, and he said, Oh, something I said? Negative, I said. And then he was like, Negative? Are you a soldier? I said, Listen to this: When you're dead is it forever? You get the picture, boy. Wolfie didn't have any reaction to that at all.

Remember when Grace's kid told Mom that his testicles hadn't descended, and he was so sad but also sort of proud that he had a thing, like a dramatic problem? And Mom said, Oh, never mind, they will! Your testicles will descend when they're good and ready! And when they do . . . hoooooo boy, watch out! Remember how we were laughing at Mom imagining Grace's kid being even more freaked out than ever thinking about some explosive activity down there when his testicles dropped—remember that?

So, yeah, I'm trying to write stuff down about our life, as per your instructions. I wrote about Dad sitting at the kitchen table in his JC Penney cotton undershirt, his head bent over his Cheerios, just emanating despair but trying to be brave, trying to smile because I'd walked into the kitchen. And Mom saying, You're suffering, and putting her arms around his hunched shoulders and holding him and he's saying, *Mensch yo, mensch yo*. And Dad begging Mom with his eyes to somehow lift him out of his agony. And Mom saying, *Ick vice, ick vice*.

November 5, 1982

We rode our bikes to Oxford. Ooolala. Wolfie says to write *cycling* to Oxford, not riding our bikes to Oxford, like we're in grade two. I was so sick and tired of riding this stupid bike. My ass was killing me. I taped a plastic bag stuffed with straw and garbage to my bike seat, but it didn't make things any better. I think if this was on a report card it would say, "Miriam is struggling in Cycling."

Remember how Mom always says "How goes the battle" when she meets anyone on the street?

Remember how in church on Easter Sunday you were supposed to greet people by saying, "The Lord has risen." And then people are supposed to respond by saying, "The Lord has risen indeed!" The first time I heard that I was so freaked out. I must have been four or five. All I knew was that normally when we went to church, we said "hello" in greeting, or maybe "good morning," and now suddenly all the adults were wandering around the vestibule repeating these bizarre words to each other. Mom tried to get me to correctly respond to some dude—he had kneeled and put his beaming face right next to mine—telling me the Lord had risen, and I just couldn't do it. I couldn't make myself say the words. I hid behind Mom and buried my face in her skirt, that green, scratchy skirt with the side zipper.

I'm writing down all these little things—they're probably clichés or stupid, but whatever. Do you think I'll soon be enjoying liquid lunches at the Algonquin Round Table, hahahaha?

In Oxford we wandered around the campus pretending to be students there. I told Wolfie I'd rather be a Dead Kennedy, like the band, and he was like, Shhhhhhh. In fact, just between you and me, I want to be a clown. I think I *am* a clown. Not because I'm funny or anything, but because I was born a clown and have to grow into my calling or something.

Wolfie definitely hates my guts now. I can tell he does not want a girlfriend who is a clown. He took off to Magdalen College, which he somehow knew was pronounced "Maudlin College," saying Oscar Wilde went there, which for some reason was funny to me. But this was the wrong reaction again, and I decided to lie down in the grass and nap while he was there. It turns out that I'd lain down in the middle of a cricket game. All these guys (not crickets!) in white were screaming and running towards me, yelling, Clear off the pitch, clear off the pitch . . . At first I thought I was dreaming about some kind of apocalypse, and my ass was so sore I couldn't move very quickly so I just crawled over to the side. I finally fell asleep under a clump of Hornbeams! They are a famous kind of tree—there was a plaque explaining that the wood of the Hornbeam is used to yoke cattle and its branches are hung on doorways on May Day to symbolize the bond of sweethearts. Then some guy from Campus Security woke me up and told me I'd be arrested for vagrancy if I didn't leave immediately, and never again to rest beneath a Hornbeam. I told him, Oh yeah, my boyfriend is around here somewhere, he's a student at Maudlin College. The guy said, I'm sure he is, away we go. As we walked away, I noticed there was blood all over my pants so at least I know the pill is working.

Now I can say I was expelled from Oxford—just like your guy, that hippie poet. The one who published a *pamphlet* about atheism and the joy of sex with as many women as you can find to have sex with, even when you're married to one of the greatest writers of all time. I wandered around the City of Dreaming Spires (which is what they call Oxford—what does it mean?) looking for tampons before remembering that Wolfie had all our money i.e., barely any. I went back to the front gate and waited for him to show up and am writing this to you now. Remember you asked me to make lists of words that were in and of themselves questions asking why? I honestly don't know what you mean by that, but I've tried to start. Blood? Jesus? Cult? I made the list on the cover of my *Stateless* record so that it looked like a word bubble coming from the mouth of Lene Lovich. I wrote: *broken english, stateless, blue, nazipunksfuckoff*—which aren't even original things. That's all I could think of to write. I might spend the rest of my life trying to complete this assignment. Remember when Grace's kid asked you if you could talk? Are you okay? I mean, you know, *okay?*

I miss you so much.

Wolfie finally showed up and said we had to go to a book signing at a famous bookstore called Blackwell's. I said, No, I need tampons. But he said we were going, end of story. He couldn't believe he was going to meet one of his heroes, John Fowles. There was a super long lineup waiting to get Fowles's autograph and my panties were soaked with blood and I was trying not to pass out from hunger, and I was mad, mad, mad. I asked, What'll he sign? Your ass? And I told Wolfie, You're not buying a book, not a fuckin hardcover book, when we don't even have enough money for fuckin food right now and I'm literally bleeding out right now in this fuckin dumb town. I was so mad. People were staring at me, and the bookstore guy asked me to leave—everyone's always asking me to leave—and everyone was staring and clearing their throats. I could smell my own blood. Wolfie's hero was too old and far away to hear us fighting. But even Wolfie told me to leave and wait for him outside, and he actually threw some pounds at me and told me to go buy my shit. And I was screaming at everyone, Fuck you all and your little fuckin books all fuckin lined up and sad, fuck you!

Afterwards Wolfie said we had some soul-searching to do, and I was like, Do you think you'll find one? And he said, It's things like that. Your sarcasm. He said respect is the fourth leg on the table of relationships. Now I'm really trying not to fight with him. We're sitting in a cemetery on the edge of The Dreaming Spires. Wolfie has to re-pack his saddlebag to accommodate his new fucking hardcover book, *Mantissa*, which is about a writer who gets amnesia and winds up in a hospital where a hot nurse who is really a doctor tells him the only way he'll remember stuff is if he has a lot of sex with her because the memory and sex part of the brain is the same thing. Wolfie says it's an experimental thought exercise about writing fiction. I asked him what the writer had written to him on the front flap and W said, "From one aspiring writer to another." W said he'd asked him to write that. I asked W if he was an aspiring writer and he said, Yeah, obviously. And you're my muse. I was like, What?! I can't be your muse. You hate me! You can't hate your muse. And W said, Oh you're so cute right now, I'm going to call you Beatrice, as in Dante.

As in what the fuck is his fucking problem.

⌒

Our bikes were stolen in Rouen, where Joan of Arc was burned at the stake—so relatively speaking, we can't complain. I told W how apt it is that this town is called Ruin—something I could say because we had made a pact to never again correct each other's pronunciation of foreign words. I'm secretly rejoicing that our bikes have been stolen. We still have our records—*your* records—because they never leave our sides! Also, in Rouen I've learned about bidets and shitting into a hole in the floor of the bathroom rather than into a toilet, and W and I have resolved once again not to fight or be offended or bored, et cetera. We drew up a new agreement. First, that I was not his muse. (I hate that word.) And second, that he would learn some actual songs on his pennywhistle, and I would sway stupidly along beside him because now we really have no money. I taught him "Dirty Old Town." He still doesn't know how to blow smoke rings.

November 11? ~~1082~~. 1982.
We are hitchhiking to Paris. I have to . . . oh wait, someone has stopped their car beside us. TBC, as Mom says when she has to split.

The guy who picked us up had a nosebleed the whole time he was driving us, and he was trying to stop it with his hand and a bag and some garbage lying around the front seat. He talked non-stop in French with his hand over his face while blood trickled down his chin and onto his shirt. I kept saying, Do you want to stop? And he kept saying, *Non, non, non, c'est pas possible*. I felt like offering him a tampon to stick up his nose—but how do you say that in French?

In Paris, we were chased out of a park by two very irritable men with whistles and sashes. They were guards of the grass, and we were not allowed on it to sleep, to sit, to walk, to busk, to linger, to eat, to nothing. They also said, *Non, non, non, c'est pas possible*, like the guy with the nosebleed. Not a lot is possible in Paris, as it turns out—and as you may be surprised, as a francophile, to hear. I wanted a roasted chestnut, like in that song you and I used to sing, but W said no. He bought a hardcover medical book, and we don't have enough money for a chestnut. We stole leftover food and a half-litre of red wine from some small round tables outside a café with a yellow heat lamp and then we smashed the glass bottle on stone steps leading into the Seine. It's not sane, it's sen. It's not Thames, it's Tems. We switched from Larks to Gauloises (which I have no idea how to pronounce), which were the brand of cigarette ends we found on the ground, and we've now decided to split for Greece—like, fast, because it's getting so cold. We want to get jobs picking olives or fishing, and sleep in the hippie caves of Matala, like Joni Mitchell. I asked W if olives were fruit, or a vegetable, and he said they're just growths. We're going to take a boat from somewhere in Italy to Corfu and then to Athens and then to Crete. We're so cold and hungry now that we don't really have the strength to fight a lot. That might be one of the keys to a good relationship.

⁓

November 14, etc.
We're in a ditch—I think, in Switzerland. I'm wearing all my clothes at once. I have socks on my hands and a T-shirt tied around my head. I'm carrying the records. Wolfie is carrying our bottle of water and jar of Nutella and rock-hard baguette. That's all we have. It's really dark, and we're in the mountains. The Alps. I thought an alp was a mountain, but "the Alps" is the name of a mountain range. I was telling W about this dream I had about getting shot in the face at very close range. I don't know who shot me, and I was so mad at myself for not getting out of the way faster. I didn't feel any pain or rage, or anything like that, just anger at myself. There was a lot of blood, and my mouth was shot right off my face and went flying down a long, empty corridor. It just disappeared. W said, Your mouth? That's pretty obvious, the meaning of that. I told him I didn't want to hear his interpretation of my dream. I didn't want to be a

person with obvious dreams. I told him I'd also had a dream where I was a clown dying of thirst in the desert and I was seeing chameleons everywhere, and W said that was also obvious. He told me he'd had a dream that I was having an affair with a money-changer in Paris. I said I thought we were too young to have anything called an affair, and he said, Well, what do you call it, then? And I said, Just something that happened. W asked me, Well, did it happen? I said, In your dream it happened. Then he said, But in real life? And I was like, Do you mean while we were stealing food and being hunted in a park by those guys with whistles in Paris for six hours, did I sneak off to bang a money-lender? W said, A changer, a money-changer. Lender is from the Bible. I said, I'd rather have a thing right now with a money-lender than a money-changer—which I thought was funny because we were so broke. Like, okay I'll pay you back next week! Hahahaha! But W got mad and sped up—that's what he does, he walks fast so I have to run to keep up with him. I was mad then too, and I yelled at him, Do you know what most people say when they're dying? They call out for their mothers! I was running along beside W, and he was ignoring me. Or they say, Fuck fuck fuck shit shit. Things like that. Or they talk about needing to get on a train. Did you know that the brain continues to function, to remember things, probably good things, thirty seconds after the heart stops beating, after death. So for a good half minute, while people are screaming and sobbing all around you because you have just died, you are remembering good things. If you are alone and have just died, there will be no screaming and sobbing and you will be left in peace to remember good things for thirty seconds.

Wolfie finally stopped ignoring me to tell me I was insane. He said I had real issues. I told him, Nothing is obvious, you don't know what my dreams mean! I was really shouting, then, and I couldn't stop talking about Albert Einstein and Lord Byron abandoning their kids. I asked W if he wanted to pretend that we were Eduard and Allegra, the two crazy abandoned children of great, great men. I said, Do you? He said, I do not. He knocked me on the side of the head with his knuckles, but gently, and he said, You're all alone in there.

I did feel like I was going crazy then, and that W was right. I said, Seriously, why don't you just want to act it out, for kicks or whatever, that you're Eduard Einstein and I'm Allegra, and W said, But you'd be five and I'd be a schizophrenic teenager, and it was two different eras. I said, Who cares? Anyway, we're on our own and our parents have left us. But W doesn't want to do it with me. He doesn't want to be Eduard. So now I'm making a mental list for you of all the things I like to do alone. I like to think about why you've stopped talking; I like to smoke, get high, walk, cry, swear, panic, play, practise knots, build volcanoes, and climb trees, poles, walls, sheds, lifeguard stands, silos, utility towers, steeples, hip-roof dairy barns, tower cranes, fire escapes. Sometimes I think that if I could have been born on my own, I would have just silently placed myself between Mom and Dad while they slept. And when they woke up, I would have quietly said, in a very calm voice, Good morning, I'm here now. Don't worry about me.

Remember when Dad found that dead mother mouse behind the piano and she had just given birth prematurely because she'd been poisoned—by Dad—and there were tiny mouse fetuses still in their sacks lying there next to her body and Dad said, Oh, unsavoury. And he tried to block us from seeing them? I think about that scene two or three times a day. I don't know why. It was so fucked up, but the way Dad said "unsavoury" was so funny, and we were laughing so hard, from the shock and horror. And Dad said, What is wrong with you girls that you find this horrific scene so funny? It's just one of those things that I think about to make myself feel better. Along with the nazipunksfuckoff song. And *Blue*, my record. Your record.

I don't even know if I should write this, or if this is the kind of letter you had in mind when you told me to write you letters, but . . . I think I might be a hostage. Don't tell Mom! I'm in a huge old house somewhere in some mountains overlooking an ocean. There are no other houses around, just trees. There are also penis sculptures and penis pictures everywhere, and the lampshades are in the shape of penises too, I think. W has taken off because he asked me to marry him, and I said no. Not NO! Just no, as in: I'm way too young to get married. And also, Why do you want to get married to an insane eighteen-year-old who you hate?

I'm in this house because an Italian butcher picked us up in Switzerland and drove two hundred miles an hour through the mountains to this place, which he says belongs to his son, and he gave us two raw steaks from his trunk and two bottles of wine and then took off. I think he said he'd be back in the morning to take us to the boat to get to Corfu—but I don't know for sure.

We accidentally burned the steaks and filled the house up with smoke because we don't know how to make steaks. So then we just ate bread and Nutella and sat on this very wide windowsill with the window open, no screen, to get some fresh air and clear out the cooking smoke—and to smoke cigarettes and drink all the wine and look out at the lights of the city down below, which I think is called Ancona. And that's when Wolfie popped the question. When I said no, and he took off. He said I was a fucking piece of work (piece of work?) and has now disappeared into the woods. What do you think I should do? Sit and wait for him to come back? Go look for him? Try to walk to that town? Find a phone? Call home?

Wait, oh my god . . .

. . . I found a stereo in this dick house and I'm listening to all of my records! Your records.

November 21, 1982

A bunch of things have happened—including that Wolfie eventually came back with a peace offering of pine cones tied together with vine strings, which then I had to carry around with me. And the butcher picked us up and took us to the ferry in Brindisi, and we got on a boat to Corfu. And in Corfu we were pelted with pomegranates at the top of a mountain by a gang of children, and I lost *Stateless*, your record—the kids took it, I'm really sorry, I'm Statelessless, you're Statelessless. And we failed every morning to get up early enough to get on the boat to Athens, although eventually we made it by staying up all night in this little park where there were roosters who woke us up on time, and I cried on the bus in Athens because we had gone all the way to the post office to see if there was mail for us or money from Mom, and there wasn't. Wolfie said I was spoiled and weak and immature, which I guess is true, but it's also true that he's a fucking asshole. And an old woman was standing next to me in the aisle of the bus, and she gently patted my back because she could see I was crying, and she kept giving Wolfie dirty looks and I really wanted to go with her, to wherever she was going. I almost got off the bus with her. And right now we're starving to death in a town called Rethymno, in Crete. We're living on the beach, not where Joni Mitchell lived in caves, that's on the other side of the island, and this guy named Pantelis—which is pronounced "pantyless"—this guy who owns a perfume shop in town gave us jobs picking olives for his friend, which means that because I'm female I have to shake the branches and crawl around on my hands and knees and pick up all the olives from the tarps laid out around the trees and put them in barrels, and all Wolfie has to do is put the barrels on a truck. We went to see *Midnight Express* at this little cinema that had twelve seats, and now I'm terrified of someone planting drugs on me and being imprisoned for the rest of my life and tortured. Also, Wolfie found another book by his favourite writer, called *The Magus*, and I started reading it because it's set in Greece and it's terrifying me. I want to get rid of it somehow. I think I'm going to take all Wolfie's books and burn them on the beach. Things are really shitty now between me and W since I said I didn't want to get married. We've ditched all our pacts, we barely talk, and when we do, all we talk about is food and the money that we're trying to save to get tickets for the Magic Bus to Frankfurt to fly home. And he told me that he'd slept with (fucked) this older Polish lady who was an actress (which is where he learned about avant-garde theatre!) when he was working at that restaurant in the city, and this spurred me on to meet this guy named Giorgi in a taverna here and have sex with him on his motorcycle.

⮑

December 12, 1982

This might be my last letter. I'm on the Magic Bus alone and I don't know where the driver is going. It's dark, it's nighttime, I don't know if we're in Greece or Yugoslavia. I can see outlines of people outside in the dark, picking up sticks along the road. I fell asleep before, when it was still daytime, and I woke up alone on the bus. Wolfie's gone. Everyone is gone. Where is everyone? Where is this guy driving us? I tried to ask him, but he just shooed me back to my seat. We can't understand each other anyway. Don't tell Mom! I'm a goner, goodbye, I love you. Thank you for rescuing me that time I was naked and got wedged between the dresser and the bed doing a perfect somersault. I really love you!

Oh! I'm still alive! The driver dropped everyone off at a restaurant to eat while he went for gas, but he didn't notice me sleeping on the bus and Wolfie didn't wake me up. The driver eventually drove us back to the restaurant to pick up everyone else. We're almost in Frankfurt. Wolfie is sitting on a different seat drinking ouzo with some guy. I'm so cold. And I think we've broken up.

 I can't wait to see you. Put the coffee on! As Mom says.
 I smell really bad.
 And I still have *Blue* and *Broken English*.

# Five

April 2023
The Conversación Comité has officially dropped me, uninvited me. I haven't adequately answered the question, they tell me, and my submission has been rejected. If you look at the program online you will see my head-and-shoulders photo with a black bar through it, and the word CANCELLED.

~

January 22, 1997
Dear Marj,
I'm almost finished this book. I can feel it. It's a great feeling. It may not be a great book but it's a great feeling.

~

January 29, 1997
Dear M,
I'm *still* almost finished—maybe twenty more pages to go. I don't know if this book is good or bad. All I know is that it's almost finished. Lately I can't get the idea of having a baby

out of my head. Like Zeus. Or: I can't get the idea out of my head of having a baby. Or: I can't get the baby of an idea out of my head.

∽

January 30, 1997

Dear M,

I am still almost finished. Really, this time. One final scene, wrapping it up into a carnival, small-town, very sad, very festive, like—

∽

Feb. 4, 1997

Dear M,

I can't seem to write today. (Rodin's big hand pushing harder.)

And I guess I'll bleed soon. Too bad, I was hoping I was pregnant with Credence. Credence may never happen . . .

∽

Feb whatever, 1997

Dear M,

This book is a poor substitute for self-mutilation and murder, but it absorbs my rage well, like a gasoline-soaked rag. I want to get on a plane and fly, fly, fly, fly, fly, fly anywhere. Off the earth preferably, and into another galaxy.

Feb. 24, 1997

Dear M,

I don't know what to do. I have a terrible feeling about things, a terrible feeling—

I love you. Love is very important—it's the only comfort. I wish I could take your sadness away. I'll call you this evening.

⁓

Comité . . . Comedia. Comedy. The word "comedy" comes from the revels associated with the rites of Dionysus, the god of vegetation.

This makes me laugh. Vegetation!

"I'll bring this iron bar down on your fucking face!"

"P.S. It really was funny."

"You just stay where you are and have fun. Chow!"

And if we *don't* see life as a tragedy? *Then* how do we live?

I might have asked Wolfie that last question long ago, when he and I were lolling about on Yeats's grave at the foot of Ben Bulben, arguing.

Just fuck off, horseman, cast a cold eye and just fuck right off.

My son calls me to say that my second-youngest grandchild has finally strung three words together in a sentence. He and his partner are hugely relieved.

The sentence is: Real monkey show.

My second-youngest grandchild is a truth-teller. God help her.

But I don't have the heart to point out to her parents that her words are a sentence fragment, have fallen short of true sentencehood.

⌒

Wuther: to blow with a dull roaring sound; "encountered almost exclusively in the title of Emily Brontë's 1847 novel *Wuthering Heights.*"

I'm reminded of the wind in Anne Carson's "The Glass Essay."

> "No need now to tremble for the hard frost and the
>     keen wind.
>
> Emily does not feel them,"
> wrote Charlotte the day after burying her sister.
> Emily had shaken free.
>
> A soul can do that.
> Whether it goes to join Thou and sit on the porch
>     for all eternity
> enjoying jokes and kisses and beautiful cold spring
>     evenings,
>
> you and I will never know. But I can tell you what I
>     saw.

Nude #13 arrived when I was not watching for it.
It came at night.

Very much like Nude #1.
And yet utterly different.
I saw a high hill and on it a form shaped against
    hard air.

It could have been just a pole with some old cloth
    attached,
but as I came closer
I saw it was a human body

trying to stand against winds so terrible that the
    flesh was blowing off the bones.
And there was no pain.
The wind

was cleansing the bones.
They stood forth silver and necessary.
It was not my body, not a woman's body, it was the
    body of us all.
It walked out of the light.

I could record someone reading Carson's poem, or a passage from Brontë's book, in the Wuther room of my Wind Museum. Or maybe these words could be read simultaneously, building towards . . . "The little raw soul."

Why does wind move sideways?

The explanation—as I recently read online—is that "THE EARTH IS ROTATING, and the observer rotates with it."

Real monkey show.

I find the caps in the explanation of the wind's movement funny. The words have been put in caps not by me but by the author of the explanation. Can you imagine?

The Author of the Explanation.

Author. Explanation. Platform. Ledger. Ledge. Bleach. Razor. Seine.

⁓

Was my sister's silence an attempt to translate something? Something that couldn't be said? Something that would cause too much pain if it were to be said? By saying nothing was she also *not* telling us that she wanted to die? Or did the silence convey the pain? Was that the wish? Was there a wish?

⁓

My father had a heart attack at school, in his classroom, his favourite place, a world where he made sense to himself, a world bustling with excited eleven-year-olds, a few weeks before Christmas while standing on a ladder hanging elaborate decorations, lights, mistletoe, celebrating the miracle of the birth of a saviour, his saviour.

He felt something. He knew his heart was giving out, up on that aluminum ladder, streamers all around him, and he climbed down and went to his desk and sat quietly, unnoticed, while his young students carried on with the decorating. He sat, in excruciating pain and smiling, looking on, nodding his approval, thumbs up! Until the lunch bell rang and the kids cleared out of the room. He walked home, the same cracked sidewalks he'd been walking for forty years, and lay in his bed. He waited for the heart attack to pass. He had thirty-five minutes before he'd be needed back at school. He lost consciousness. When he didn't show up for the first class after lunch break his friend, a custodian at the school, went to the house to check on him and then called an ambulance.

My father never returned to his classroom. But his body survived for another few years. He came home from the hospital, finally, with my mother, on Christmas Eve. The house was cold and dark, uninhabited for a month while my mother stayed in the city at his bedside.

My father had decorated his classroom beautifully and never was in it again. He was no longer a teacher, no longer— in his words—alive. The lights had gone out. But we, his daughters, continued to learn from him.

"All language is . . . silence."
—Maurice Merleau-Ponty

All silence is language.

Was my sister's silence holding on to something vital?

Was her silence a flirtation? A first step? An experiment? (Dead people don't talk.)

Writing isn't talking. Writing is also non-talking.

Consciousness, experience, existence. In silence, was my sister able to begin to ask herself questions?

Why live?

Why die?

What was she holding on to? Why would it be called withholding?

"The refusal to give something that is due or desired"; "To hold back, restrain or check."

But why should she talk? To risk telling lies, to be misunderstood, to lose consciousness, to give away her self. Why shouldn't she be silent?

Why do you not have children? Why do you not have a job? Why do you not get out of bed on certain days? Why are you not married? Why do you laugh at inappropriate times? Why do you argue? Why do you blow one way and then the other? Why do you cancel plans and close your curtains during the day? Why do you walk the city's empty streets at night? Why do you not believe in God? Why do you not tell other people of your plans? Why do you disappear to the coast, to the sea, to the mountains? Why do you not speak?

Why did the psychiatrist, in the last days before my sister died, refuse to see her if she wouldn't speak? What harm was she causing? What was she holding on to?

For dear life.

It's true that when she was silent, the attention of we who loved her was attuned to her.

When will she speak, why isn't she speaking, what will finally make her speak, will it be anything, what will be the words she needs to give breath to, the first words out of her mouth, why must she talk?

∽

If silence says more, why write?

# Six

Why do I write?

Because she asked me to.

~

My sister asked me for all sorts of things. To write her letters, to help her live, to help her die, to understand, to try to understand, to stop trying to understand, to let her go, to go away, to come back, to make lists, to race to the pharmacy while she bled out in that weird shag-carpeted bathroom of our old house on the highway in that freaky town in the exact middle, the very heart (so it says on a giant billboard) of the continent.

Why would I go to the navel of the universe when I can go to its heart?

On that island where my family went for a picnic so long ago, and from where our boat disappeared, we stood, the four of us, in a straight line, our hands like visors, as though saluting an unseen major general. We were stranded, marooned, the only inhabitants on this spit of land, each of us gazing out over the water, and laughing—my mother laughed first, of course, and then each of us in turn, until the wind generated by our laughter turned itself into . . . what . . . a derecho? A haboob? A powerful wind that pushed our little aluminum boat into view, suddenly, violently, bobbing on the waves, and then, as our laughter grew louder, pushed the boat, with great force, right up onto the sand where we stood. We were saved. But we were disappointed. We became quiet.

Winds change, said my father, softly. His words were almost a whisper, but they had the force of the Coriolis effect.

The Coriolis effect was discovered by Gaspard-Gustave de Coriolis in 1832, and by the end of the nineteenth century had become a common term in meteorological literature. It is classified as a "fictitious force" applied to objects that are in rotation. If individuals are spinning to the left along their y-axis and then push their head forward, this will bring their head out of alignment, making them subject to the Coriolis force. The manifestation of this effect is that the individuals will feel like their head is tilting to the left. This can cause nausea, disorientation, and motion sickness. These feelings of discomfort arise in the body when the signals being sent by the vestibular system and visual system are not in agreement, i.e., the eyes may be telling the body that one is not moving, but the vestibular system's fine-tuned senses are detecting and communicating the opposite.

This effect is a concern for airplane pilots because it can cause extreme disorientation. It happens as pilots accelerate their aircraft and need to check their instruments, which often involves moving the head. An airborne pilot might feel as if they are pitching, yawing and rolling simultaneously. In extreme situations, this can cause the pilot to lose control of the aircraft.

A description of the Coriolis force will definitely appear in my museum. But how to simulate the effect?

Our boat comes back. We are saved. We pile into the boat and drift away from the island. I'm bailing to beat the band, as my father would have said—our little boat has taken on water and I use my hands, a chipped bowl, a tin cup and a half-empty peanut butter jar, while my sister sits serenely, silently, in the prow of the sinking boat.

We're going home. We're hoping to make it. We're writing, we're bailing, we're flailing, we're sucking air, hollering into the wind, help, we're sinking. We're writing. We're bailing.

We're silent, we've made a decision. We're content. We're sitting calmly in the prow of the little boat that is definitely taking on more water now, more than before. We are not bailing. We're trying to go home. We're all trying to get home.

My sister punctuated her life with long periods of silence. It was during these periods that she begged me to write her letters—about anything, my life, the days—and in that asking was an offering. She taught me how to stay alive. Silence and words: both are good, both are failures, both are efforts, and in that effort is where life lies—not *lies*, or maybe it does—but where it exists.

And the fragments in between are the spaces where she and I meet.

May 26, 1985

Dear Miriam,

I must say you have raised the imperative tense to new heights. I found your little commands very amusing indeed. I am "NOW WRITING" so you know your efforts have not been in vain. Actually, I would have written anyway. I have had very good intentions of writing a letter for days, if not weeks, but alas have not done it. Shame on me, but I suppose when all excuses have been exposed it is you who is lonely + not me. This is not to say I don't miss you because I miss you very much, but somehow my environment is a little more comfortable than yours, I think, i.e. not conducive to letter-writing. Enough self-chastisement for now, I hope you will agree. At least I am writing on foolscap + not on aerograms which I bought with the express purpose of writing to you but which only allow 200 words. (I thought you would prefer this.)

    Speaking of self-chastisement, you have no doubt run into the Eng. Legend of T. E. Lawrence by now. Non? Well, neither had I til this morning—this is THE Lawrence of Arabia—died 50 yrs. ago this week in a motorcycle accident in Dorset—possibly thought to have been murdered or to have committed suicide. At any rate this Eng. hero was discovered in 1968 to have been a masochist, i.e. he asked to be beaten for sexual stimulation.

    . . . I bumped into Susan M. on the street and mentioned to her that you were working as a chambermaid in a hotel in Russell Square and that you had recently discovered, in one of the twelve rooms per day you're expected to clean, a large turd in the exact middle of the bed. Her response: Twelve rooms!?

. . . The weather has been a lot better here than in London, judging from the paper. When I visit, I think I'll bring my blue jacket (yours) and also an umbrella. Anything else I should bring? I am <u>very</u> excited about the trip and can think of little else. I think I'm overdue for a little excitement. I definitely want to visit Oxford and Cambridge and the sea somewhere.

. . . Alors, I'll see you in London on the 20$^{th}$ A.M. with bells on. I remember how exciting it is to touch down + hope someone from the crowd sees you because you certainly can't find anyone in the mob.

. . . Well, I hope this will make up for my silence. I'll try to write again before I leave, though I must say life goes on as usual here without too much to report. Lessons (teaching), French classes, cook, eat, clean, sleep etc. . . . I very much miss being able to call you anytime or just come over + hang out. A sister's place is in many ways even better than a friend's—you're always welcome, don't have to make arrangements etc etc. Can stay long or short, clean out the fridge, read the paper etc. In short, not be on one's best behaviour.

Well, I'm running out of space. So long + see you soon.

Love, M

I was alone.

It was late in the evening, very dark, the stars and the moon obscured—in fact, there was zero visibility, as Lisa Cook might have said during her traffic report—and I was driving east on the Trans-Canada Highway towards the Red River Valley, my home, in a whiteout blizzard.

Do you know the song *Just remember the Red River Valley? And the girl who has loved you so true?*

I was somewhere between Moose Jaw and Swift Current. It wasn't zero *zero* visibility, which means I could see, barely, the blurry red glow of the tail lights of the car in front of me, and I was determined not to lose sight of them or I'd lose my bearings and certainly hit the ditch. The car in front of me—or maybe it was a truck or a combine or a thresher, who knows—was following the red glow of the tail lights of the car in front of *it*, and so on and so on. Somewhere up ahead there must have been a person, or people—the first car in our convoy—who could see more of the road, maybe, and we were following that car. We were all driving slowly, close together. There might have been two feet between each of our cars, it's hard to say, and who knows how many cars there were ahead of me or behind me, but we had to be very close together in order to see the tail lights in front. At least we were still on the road. If there were cars in the ditch, we couldn't see them. I was intensely focused on the red dots in front of me.

Suddenly, an explosion of light and sound came at me, was on top of me. It was terrifying, blinding light, a mighty roar of something, an engine, God, I don't know. I didn't scream. I didn't say anything. I thought, *No*. And then it was gone. The blinding light, the roar. And I was back in ordinary darkness, the whiteout blizzard, zero visibility, squinting at the tail lights in front of me, focused and determined to get out of this bullshit alive.

The next day I read in the newspaper that the pilot of a cargo plane called a Dreamlifter was caught in the blizzard and became disoriented due to the zero but not quite zero visibility and was unable to distinguish the sky from the ground. He was afraid he'd crash. He decided to fly low along the highway and follow the headlights of the cars, the convoy I was a part of, on the Trans-Canada. So long as the headlights were beneath him, he reasoned, he'd be okay. We were travelling in opposite directions, of course, our convoy and the Dreamlifter. But to make out the headlights he had to fly very close above our cars—barely above our cars. We might have been able to open our windows and reach out and skim our fingers along the bottom of the Dreamlifter flying over us. It was this pilot, and his plane, the Dreamlifter, that had whooshed over us, going in the opposite direction, hoping to fly out of the storm and find a place to land.

When I told my mother about this, she said, Well, of all things. What do you know!

Then she asked me if I wanted to grab some lunch at the new Thai place on the corner.

But Mom, I said, what happened was crazy!

What can I say? she replied. That's winter driving for you.

First order of the day. (Clean up the blood.)

To write. (This strange non-thing.)

Poste restante. (Do you love this old-fashioned idea?)

Silence. Suicide. Writing. Within all of these, we are holding.

Does her silence hold the perfect expression of her suffering?

Is her silence a communications success, my writing a failure?

Are writing and suicide related? The same thing? Or estranged relatives, at least? Angry siblings whose origins are the same. An attempt—a fragment of an attempt—to save life, preserve life, to freeze it in a moment, to end what is real, to survive by ending. To preserve, in silence, what is authentic.

Writing is artifice and silence is truth. No? Well, yes. No?

But writing is life, listen to me, you clown, you don't quit, you don't grimace and wave away your audience, tell them the show is over. Writing is life and silence is the final step before the metal rail, the sharp scent of creosote, the wind.

Why must I draw a comparison between writing and suicide?

To stay with her. To stay with them.

Yes, you can imagine my suffering. Yeah, you fucking can. Try! Stay with me.

That's easy! (Remembering my mother's response to my question about why they—my father, my sister—went silent.)

It was something they could control. (They could control the beginning of not-being?)

After my cellphone-in-the-river episode, the breakdown,

the torn coat lining, the madness, the divorce, the sickness, my sister's silence, the dread, here we go again: the only thing I can control is the writing. Or, the only *other* thing I can control, the only alternative to doing away with myself, as they (who?) say.

I will go there with you. I will go right to the very edge of the rail where you can smell the creosote, feel the limestone shale give way under your feet—or is it ballast?—a small earth quaking.

And: good news! Or: good news for my museum. The Chinese have discovered how to capture the wind created by trains as they whoosh down the track. They do this with small devices installed on the undercarriages. The captured wind then drives a turbine to generate electricity.

The immense altering of silence, of writing. It is the same. We are sisters. We are thieves. We steal ourselves, and others, and we alter them, Frankenstein them, ourselves, into something that tracks, that scans, that makes sense, that remains. Something not corporeal, this strange non-thing.

But being alive is worth something.

Why do you write?

Why do you live?

⁍

"And yet I've come to believe, and in rare moments can almost feel, that like an illness some vestige of which the body keeps to protect itself, pain may be its own reprieve; that the violence that is latent within us may be, if never altogether dispelled or tamed, at least acknowledged, defined, and perhaps by dint of the love we feel for our lives, for the people in them and for our work, rendered into an energy that need not be inflicted on others or ourselves, an energy we may even be able to use; and that for those of us who have gone to war with our own minds there is yet hope for what Freud called 'normal unhappiness,' wherein we might remember the dead without being haunted by them, give to our lives a coherence that is not 'closure,' and learn to live with our memories, our families, and ourselves amid a truce that is not peace."

—Christian Wiman

⁓

I recently returned from Winnipeg, where I sat on my son's front porch in the west end of that city. Warm wind. Hot wind. Red sky. Music coming from inside. My son in the kitchen making us eggs and toast.

I should get flowers and go to her grave, I thought. I should.

My son's partner told me that my son had learned, from me, not to have needs.

I objected. She amended, telling me I had to go small as a kid, to take care of others, or at least not be in any way a burden, invisible.

Fine . . . this is true. But I did write books, I told her. And so does he, my son. Surely that's a need?

Before I had arrived in Winnipeg, I'd been in Hollywood. I met a movie star there. She asked me what I did. I told her I was a writer. She said, Oh that's so sweet!

I lost my voice in Hollywood. Or, in any case, it disappeared. I phoned the front desk at my hotel to order room service and discovered I had lost my ability to speak. I hung up. Tried again. Hung up.

The front desk receptionist called my room. I picked up the phone and breathed.

Is there a problem? the receptionist asked.

I tried to tell her no, no, not at all. But: nothing, silence.

E was with me. We rented a car and drove as fast as we could away from Hollywood, down the coast to a town called San Clemente. We rented an Airbnb close to the beach. We opened the wrong garage door and parked our rental car inside. The owner of the garage drove up and asked us why we had parked our car inside his garage.

We're sorry, said E. We're Canadians. The owner of the garage nodded, suspicious but calm. What do you do up in Canada?

I still had no voice. E looked at me. I shook my head. We removed our car from the man's garage and vigorously waved goodbye.

In Winnipeg, I played with my granddaughters. The six-year-old was the Queen and she named me Princess Lisa. (Why am I always Lisa?) Her three-year-old sister was the King.

The Queen and the King sat side by side in tiny chairs. The Queen wore an elaborate gown and tiara. The King, clad in a diaper and nothing else, clutched a stuffed mouse. They both had wands. The King and I have been talking, said the Queen. (The King talks?) And we've decided that you must do more work around here!

But I'm a princess! I said. Princesses don't work.

Yes! said the Queen. They do! You will! There's a hurricane coming, and you must go and warn the villagers and give them these manuals showing them how to survive a hurricane!

The Queen got up and carried her King to the bookshelf. She grabbed books from the lower shelf and threw them into a pile on the floor. These are your manuals! Take them to the villagers! Now! She threw a stuffed hobby horse at me. Hurry!

The manuals had titles such as:

*All That Is Solid Melts Into Air: The Experience of Modernity*
*The Origins of Totalitarianism*
*The Berkeley Student Revolt: Facts and Interpretations*
*The Organizer's Manual*
*Occupy! Scenes from Occupied America*

As I hastened to the village, the Queen continued to holler about saving lives while her King launched into a wordless rendition of "Row, Row, Row Your Boat."

Back home in Toronto, I dreamed that I had three small children. Some other people in my dream were insisting on naming my children. Their names would be Rachel, something else I can't remember, and Henry.

No! I said in my dream. Those aren't their names!

I didn't know what the names of my children *were*, but I knew these weren't their names.

Those aren't their names!

Yes, the people insisted, calmly, authoritatively. Those are their names.

⁓

Every two or three months I need to affirm a narrative for my mother: that she was not a failure, that she did everything she could, that she couldn't have saved my father and my sister in the end, that she had to survive and remain and breathe, for the rest of us, for herself, for me.

But of course, this narrative is not necessarily *true*. What's true is that she chose to remain.

A little while ago, on the thirteenth anniversary of my sister's death, my mother and I talked about the day my sister died. My sister had been given a weekend pass from the hospital in Winnipeg. It was a Saturday. The next day was my sister's birthday, and we were planning a small party, just family, with cake and gifts.

On that Saturday, the day my sister had been allowed to go home, my mother stopped in at her house to say hello. Nobody was home but the door was unlocked, wide open.

How strange. Eventually my mother left to meet a friend and have lunch. She told her friend, "I honestly don't know if she's dead or alive."

When my mother and I talked about that day, my mother said, finally, and for the first time, It's been a rough life.

My mother: I can still smell the bleach on her breath. She reached up to me. She held her arms open.

My mother: I wish he (my sister's partner) had properly cleaned her blood off the floor. Still on the tiles, still, see?

Silence and writing are, if not quite the same thing, then allies—each a misdirection of the unspeakable, and each a way of holding on.

My sister to me: You're a survivor.

But of what, and in relation to what? To herself? *She* was a survivor.

What did she mean?

"It can be a relief to release one's hold on singularity for the sake of a binding truth, even if the truth is only that there can be no such thing. If we can't salvage the bits of memory and matter that have made us what we are, let us at least acknowledge the whirlwind."

—Christian Wiman

My grandson to my mother: Great-grandma, a narwhal can die of fear.

No, honey, said my mother. It can't.

Yes, Great-grandma, it can.

There are forest fires burning everywhere these days, hundreds of them, and the wind is fanning the flames and blowing the ashes across the world, and the skies over Toronto and the entire continent are filled with smoke and tiny particles of something or other which, we are warned, can kill us, and we must stay inside our houses and close the windows and do our best to keep our breathing tracts open.

My mother hasn't heard the warnings. Or she's ignored them. She has set off with her walker towards a neighbourhood blocks and blocks away, over a bridge, across the tracks, past the derelict slaughterhouse now inhabited by feral cats. Where has she gone? We clearly didn't manage to convey the warnings to her. She's barely able to walk a few blocks without becoming short of breath and needing to sit and rest. The sky is charcoal grey. The CN Tower is blurry. The streets are empty.

We wait for her to come home—and she does at last, exhilarated. She has done it, she has made it. And what a beautiful day! she says. I met so many interesting people along the way.

Really? I say. But isn't everyone staying inside?

My grandkids all have magic wands—in fact, "multiple wand options," as the eldest puts it. We'll be fine, they say. We have many magic wands.

The deranged skunk has come back. An official from the City told us she might be pregnant and looking to secure a birthing shelter. But how do you know it's a female? I asked. Oh, we know. We just know.

The skunk comes back every night now. Clawing and pawing away at the outside of the concrete wall next to my mother's bedroom. The city official told us it's "memory muscle." The skunk used to live here with her family, before everything went wrong, and she became deranged. There's no way she can get in there now. Soon she'll die from exhaustion. She won't stop.

I remember how once, when I was on a book tour in Germany, my editor there insisted on buying two large stuffed mice for me to take home to my grandchildren. I only had two grandchildren then. My suitcase was very small. I told my editor I didn't have enough room in my suitcase and that it would be awkward to traipse around Europe on my book tour with giant stuffed mice. But she insisted that I take them back to my grandkids.

I left a chunky sweater and a pair of shoes behind in Cologne in order to cram the mice into my suitcase. I travelled all over Germany and Italy with them. My bag was checked by suspicious airport security people who asked me why I was travelling from city to city with these mice and little else. I left yet more clothing behind in hotels along the way, plus a hairbrush and my deodorant and a few books that were taking up room. Eventually, I was carrying only a couple of pairs of underwear and a T-shirt and my toothbrush. And by the time I got home I'd got rid of absolutely everything except the mice.

I remember lifting my suitcase up and into the overhead bin of the last plane, the one that would take me home, finally. It was so light and easy! A very gentle wind could have, without any difficulty, picked up my suitcase and carried it off to god knows where—which, I think now, might be something to demonstrate in my Wind Museum. In fact, I recall now that when my suitcase contained only the mice, it *had* been pushed by the wind on the tarmac, about twenty metres or so. I ran after it yelling, Stop, stop. It zigged and zagged, and I pursued it in my floppy shoes, getting close, closer, until it was within inches of my grasp, but then away it went again, taken by the wind, rolling, and I ran again, drenched in sweat, calling out for my luggage to stop, please, now.

And it's true, a few people, a family that was watching, laughed, and I was so grateful—I'd created a *bit,* and the best part of the bit, the punchline, was revealed at the end when I finally caught my suitcase, pinned it down to the tarmac and opened it, for my audience of four, revealing its ridiculous contents, just two orange stuffed mice that had almost given me a heart attack, had left me struggling to breathe, had made it look as though I was fighting for my very life, in Bari, Southern Italy, near Ancona, near that strange house in the hills where so many years ago I'd finally been able to play the records I'd stolen from my sister.

꿈

I also remember August 16, 1977. A momentous day. I was thirteen, visiting family in La Chorrera, Panama.

This was the day I saw my cousin's balls. I'd never seen balls before. Also, Elvis died, and I made myself understood in another language when I asked for a litre of milk in Spanish.

When I told my missionary aunt and uncle that the King was dead, they said, Shhhhh, no, and shooed me out of the room.

⁓

I have a plan for retirement, I tell my kids. I'm gonna be happy for the next twenty years, and then I'll kill myself.

It doesn't work that way! they say.

Yes, I say. It does!

⁓

"I thought about Ulysses, the man whose great deed was nothing more or less than getting home, and I went on my way."

—Juan Villoro

⁓

I think of my mother's words to me one morning recently, on the subject of bowel movements:

When I was young, and when I first understood the importance of bowel movements, I was always constipated. All my life, all my life. Until I got married, then I stopped being constipated. Now, I have one bowel movement a week.

Me: Why do you think you stopped being constipated when you got married?

My mother: I think because I had a home.

I remembered then how she'd been on her own from the age of fifteen onwards, after her mother died and her older brothers sent her away to be a maid in America.

What came first? I asked her. You needed a home, so you married Dad and were then able to have a bowel movement? Or you fell in love with Dad and got married, and then, as it happened, you had a home and were able to have a bowel movement?

∽

"I managed to get him to talk to me about his new favorite malady. At the end of the nineteenth century, the French psychiatrist Jules Cotard diagnosed this 'negation delirium,' a special variation of melancholy in which the sick person takes on an absolute and defensive negation. Isolated from all responsibility, the patient defends himself from the outside and dynamites his language, trying to express himself through the strange path of verbal impoverishment. In this way, he protects himself. Transformed into nothing, he cannot be affected: he lacks lack. The apocalypse has already occurred, and he survives without hope."

—Juan Villoro

I've bought a shirt that says in bold Gothic letters: *I've come to do the devil's work.*

I know it's silly and immature. My daughter wonders aloud if perhaps I shouldn't wear it when I pick up my grandson from daycare. But I am pleased with this shirt.

∽

I think about how, many years ago, decades ago, I lied to my German artist friend and told her I was a professional whistler. I said that I would easily be able to whistle along with Yo-Yo Ma in concert.

My friend believed me and developed a show where I would do just that. She brought me Yo-Yo Ma CDs so that I could practise. I didn't know how to tell her I'd been lying.

Eventually I confessed that I was not a professional whistler, but that it had been my life's dream to become one.

Life's dream.

∽

I think about the strangeness of the old white bearded man I met at a university book fair in La Paz, who pointed at me, angrily, hatefully, saying my name in the original Mennonite language: "Toyfs."

How did he know me? Why was he there?

I had seen him before, I realized. Or others like him, so many others.

I mentioned this to the young woman responsible for getting me from place to place at the fair. She didn't understand what I was telling her. We spoke different languages. But she sensed that I was nervous. *Qué pasa?* she said. *Tienes miedo?*

~

I think about our little house in Toronto, which caused such consternation for my neighbours, and how it sits on top of an underground river that starts somewhere up around St. Clair Avenue and ends in Lake Ontario. The river is underground now, but it wasn't always. As York grew, hundreds of years ago, the river became polluted and the City decided to bury the river in an underground sewer, which continues to flow today. Directly under our house. Now our sump pump works constantly, twenty-four hours a day, to prevent our home from filling up with water and drowning us in our beds, from floating away. I can feel moisture on the basement walls. There are cracks in those walls. I think about our angry ex-neighbours, how they'll have the last laugh when this river of tears wins, finally, unburies itself and carries us off to sea.

Meanwhile, my mother, halfway down the long driveway, says to me, Hey, watch this!

I look over at her and she starts running! She's running towards me with surprisingly good form, arms and legs moving in synch, a fierce, determined look on her face. I can't believe what I'm seeing.

Oh, I can run, she tells me. Running's no problem. I just can't breathe.

My mother has an eye infection. When she sleeps, her eyes are glued shut with green pus. One morning when I checked on her, she was talking quietly in her sleep. I listened closely.

She said, "Why?"

Then, softly, "SOS."

I touched her arm. I took her hand. She woke up, but her eyes didn't open.

How are you? I asked.

Oh, fine! she said.

That afternoon, my mother warned my son-in-law: Don't be alarmed if I scream in my sleep.

⁓

This morning, I found a lightsaber in my mother's bed.

And now we find ourselves, my old mother and I, playing "Keep It Up" with a balloon left over from one of the kids' birthday parties. This is long after the kids have quit the game, a game they initiated, and left the room.

There's a gentle wind—no, not a wind, a breeze, or not even a breeze, only air moving softly through the window screen into the room, enough to move the balloon around a bit sometimes so that we just miss it, our aim is off, and we have to scramble to get it and make sure it doesn't hit the floor, and we're committed to this now, to the game, this kids' game, we two old grandmas with no kids in the room.

We play together for a long, long time, with the soft air coming through the window screen—a third playmate, a wafting playmate, is this soft air—and eventually the kids come back into the room and my older grandson says, the way he does, What the . . . !

Earlier this morning I found blood on my mother's sheet. Where is this from? I asked her, thinking back to her *first order of the day*.

But she laughed. Oh . . . yeah . . . she said vaguely. Listen, we're in a hurry, let's go!

Now I'm thinking that my Wind Museum needs a room like this: a room with a balloon in it, a balloon that appears to be batted about, gently, but with enough force and precision that it never touches the floor. There would be no people in the room other than the museum guest who is watching the balloon, and possibly feeling, barely, the soft air coming through a screen. Everything else would be left to their imagination.

Who is batting this balloon around? Who is in the room, keeping the balloon from falling to the floor? Who is there? Nobody is there.

Then, maybe, the museum guest will think, Well, I'm here. Am I alone?

I think about my mother at her cardiologist's office, how she and the doctor joke, hold hands, talk about her ticker, her imminent death, laugh.

The doctor will go to her computer to look at concerning ECG results, kidney results. Not too hot, she will say.

Oh, she knows, my mother does, and she will laugh again and thank her cardiologist for her care all these years. Then she'll open her Simenon book and read, coolly absorbed, while the doc pulls up her numbers.

~

And now, it is Christmas. A curtain rod has fallen, narrowly missing my mother's head. She roars with laughter, grabs the rod and uses it as a lightsaber (Aha!) as she joins the younger grandkids in a game of "Attack and Die." Meanwhile, there's a leak in my mother's washroom, and the plumber arrives and asks how many people live here, exactly?

The wall is sawed open, and the children watch, amazed. Pipes in the walls! My second-youngest grandchild has thrown part of the back-door handle down the vent. How will we enter and exit? The coffee maker explodes and a baseboard in the kitchen peels away and is employed as a weapon; the basement door comes off its hinges and books are used to build a temporary barricade to keep the little ones from tumbling down the stairs. My second-youngest grandchild throws my mother's expired nitro spray down the vent. The stereo is definitely, permanently fucked. I think of *Broken English*, of *Blue*. The backyard has turned to mud from the children's new toy roller coaster. A cardboard box "tunnel" has been destroyed in the rain. Mice are back in the house, with a vengeance, and the lights in the dining and living rooms are now flickering constantly as the children upstairs stomp, stomp, stomp. Three balls and a diaper are stuck in the Christmas tree branches, too high to reach, and my mother is strung out on oxys, because her trigeminal neuralgia is back. She says her new hearing aids are amazing, though, and she watched a Raptors game at three in the morning and could clearly hear my son's voice commentating during the first half. But not the second. Where did he go for the second half? Everyone has colds, and stomach issues, and all the children have lightsaber injuries, as does their aunt, who has a scratched cornea and now must wear a patch and so, in solidarity, must we all. The children's fiat! We are patched!

⁓

December 25, 2023

Dear Marj,
My second-eldest grandchild gave me his Christmas list today! It's a bit late. And I'm trying to make out the words.

> A crab stuffie
> A yo-yo
> My own army

(I thought you'd like that.)
And this, you'll like this: A perfect stranger walked into the house—teeming with chaos as usual—last night around dinnertime. A few of us saw him come into the house and assumed he'd been invited to spend Christmas Eve with us, but by whom? Maybe he was an old friend of my mother's?

A former professor of one of my kids? A great-uncle of my daughter-in-law? We called out to him, Welcome, c'mon in! He sat down on the stairs and took off his snowy boots and hung up his coat on a hook and came into the kitchen, smiling, though somewhat tentative. We said, Hello! Merry Christmas! And we gave him a drink and ushered him into the living room. The toddlers crawled all over him and smacked him a few times and knocked his glasses off; and the older kids forced him to play "Rock, Paper, Scissors" without end, and insisted that he tell them all his jokes, as if every stranger who wanders into one's home is a comedian with a repertoire of ready material; and we adults made polite conversation about the weather and the holidays, glancing at each other, discreetly, for some kind of clue or hint as to who this guy was.

Finally, twenty minutes into his visit, he said, You know, you people are so kind, but I do believe I'm in the wrong house. Does a Rocco live here?

～

"Whether it goes to join thou and sit on the porch
    for all eternity
enjoying jokes and kisses and beautiful cold spring
    evenings,

You and I will never know. But I can tell you what I
    saw."

My mother remembers, suddenly, that today is her wedding anniversary.

Now my grandchildren re-enact her wedding and dance elegantly, with great feeling. They don't know, of course, that there was no dancing at my mother's wedding. Or that dancing, in general, was strictly forbidden in the community, a surefire path to hell.

My mother cries as she watches the children waltz, with comic formality, around the room. She applauds and they bow and curtsey, falling over each other, tripping on toys and lightsabers and fighting for centre stage.

"And there was no pain.
The wind

was cleansing the bones.
They stood forth silver and necessary.
It was not my body, not a woman's body, it was the
    body of us all.
It walked out of the light."

My son brings out a framed photo of my mother and father, both aged twenty-one. It is their wedding photo. My son puts it in the centre of the table.

My youngest grandson sits at the table, alone, and stares at the photo intently with his one unpatched eye while the house falls down around him and my mother shuffles to her bedroom, puts on her wedding dress, which she has kept all this time in its original box, and dances with the children, until her angina acts up and she exclaims, Oh, phooey!

This delights the children, who have never heard this word before, and they shout it out a thousand times while my mother sits and breathes. Then, after much consultation among the children, she is given the task of keeping score for the world's most epic lightsaber battle.

We all pause for a moment, silent, before it begins.

PERMISSIONS AND ACKNOWLEDGEMENTS

The author gratefully acknowledges the words of all writers quoted in these pages.

The title of this work, *A Truce That Is Not Peace*, comes from Christian Wiman's "The Limit," from *Ambition and Survival: Becoming a Poet* (Copper Canyon Press, 2007).

Excerpt from "The Limit" from *Ambition and Survival: Becoming a Poet*, copyright © 2007 by Christian Wiman. Reprinted by permission of Copper Canyon Press, coppercanyonpress.org.

Excerpt from *Survival Is a Style: Poems* by Christian Wiman. Copyright © 2020 by Christian Wiman. Reprinted by permission of Farrar, Straus and Giroux. All Rights Reserved.

Excerpt from *Little Snow Landscape* by Robert Walser, trans. Tom Whalen, copyright © 2021 by Tom Whalen. Reprinted by permission of New York Review Books.

Excerpt from "The Glass Essay" by Anne Carson, from *Glass, Irony and God*, copyright ©1995 by Anne Carson. Reprinted by permission of New Directions Publishing Corp.

Excerpts from *Horizontal Vertigo: A City Called Mexico* by Juan Villoro, copyright © 2021 by Juan Villoro. Published by Vintage, an imprint of Knopf Doubleday and division of Penguin Random House LLC. All rights reserved.

Excerpts from *Dear Friend, from My Life I Write to You in Your Life* by Yiyun Li, copyright © 2017 by Yiyun Li. Used by permission of Random House, an imprint and division of Penguin Random House LLC. All rights reserved.

The passage that appears on pages 80-93 of this book is a substantially edited and modified version of a personal essay by the author that appeared in the *New Yorker* ("The Way She Closed the Door," February 7, 2022).

For ongoing support of my writing life, thank you to my agent Sarah Chalfant at The Wylie Agency and my editor Lynn Henry at Knopf Canada.

WORKS CITED

*In order of appearance*

Wiman, Christian. "The Limit." In *Ambition and Survival: Becoming a Poet*. Port Townsend, WA: Copper Canyon Press, 2004.

Chekhov, Anton. "The Steppe." In *The Steppe and Other Stories, 1887–91*, translated by Ronald Wilks. London, UK: Penguin Classics, 2005.

Wiman, Christian. *Survival Is a Style*. New York, NY: Farrar, Straus and Giroux, 2020.

Savage, Sam. *The Cry of the Sloth*. Minneapolis, MN: Coffee House Press, 2009.

Walser, Robert. *Little Snow Landscape*. Translated by Tom Whalen. New York, NY: New York Review Books, 2021.

Li, Yiyun. *Dear Friend, from My Life I Write to You in Your Life*. New York, NY: Random House, 2017.

Camus, Albert. *The Myth of Sisyphus and Other Essays.* New York, NY: Alfred A. Knopf, 1955.

Kerouac, Jack. *On the Road.* New York, NY: Viking Press, 1957.

Carson, Anne. "The Glass Essay." In *Glass, Irony, and God.* New York, NY: New Directions, 1995.

Merleau-Ponty, Maurice. "Indirect Language and the Voices of Silence." In *Signs*, edited by John Wild, translated by Richard C. McCleary. *Studies in Phenomenology and Existential Philosophy.* Evanston, IL: Northwestern University Press, 1964.

Wiman, Christian. "The Drift of the World." *POETRY*, June 2020.

Villoro, Juan. *Horizontal Vertigo: A City Called Mexico.* Translated by Alfred MacAdam. New York, NY: Pantheon, 2021.

A NOTE ON THE AUTHOR

MIRIAM TOEWS is the author of the internationally acclaimed and bestselling novels *Fight Night*, *Women Talking*, *All My Puny Sorrows*, *Irma Voth*, *The Flying Troutmans*, *A Complicated Kindness*, *A Boy of Good Breeding*, and *Summer of My Amazing Luck*, and one prior work of non-fiction, *Swing Low: A Life*. She is the winner of numerous awards, including the Governor General's Literary Award for Fiction, the Libris Award for Fiction, Canada Reads, the Writers' Trust Fiction Prize, and the Writers' Trust Engel Findley Award. She lives in Toronto.